CONTEMPORARY
CABLES

Classic Aran Reimagined in Current Styles

Jody Long

DOVER PUBLICATIONS, INC.
Mineola, New York

DEDICATION

*This book is dedicated to my mum and dad
for always encouraging me!*

ACKNOWLEDGMENTS

I would like to say a big thank you to all of the following:

To my wonderful commissioning editor Katharine Maller, for allowing me to write this book, and to Vanessa Putt, my new editor, who kept me on my toes and helped me to finish this book.

To my dad, Tony Long, for art directing and taking the photos.

To the fabulous models, Joseph Johns and Cara Louise Partridge, who no doubt will never forget the photo shoot, as we all battled the cold sea air and carried on regardless of what Mother Nature threw at us that day!

To my fantastic knitters, Karen Evans, Rita Taylor, Susan Winn, Tina Miller, Josephine Lockwood, Marcy Spavins, Rachel Wiseman, Linda Barker, and Hetty Williams.

Models: Joseph Johns and Cara Louise Partridge
Photographer: Tony Long

Bibliographical Note

Contemporary Cables: Classic Aran Reimagined in Current Styles is a new work,
first published by Dover Publications, Inc., in 2017.

International Standard Book Number

ISBN-13: 978-0-486-80527-6
ISBN-10: 0-486-80527-1

Manufactured in the United States by LSC Communications
80527101   2017
www.doverpublications.com

CONTEMPORARY
CABLES

CONTENTS

Garter and Cable Sweater
8

Mock Turtleneck Pullover
12

Cropped Boxy Cardigan
18

Men's Two-Color Pullover
24

Rapunzel Sweater
30

Oversized Wrap
40

Market Tote
44

Sweater Dress
48

Men's Crewneck Pullover
56

Crossover Shrug
62

Men's Shawl Collar Pullover
66

Buttonless Chunky Cardigan
72

Diamond Cabled Pullover
78

Cabled Beret
84

Tunic Sweater
88

Grandfather Cardigan
94

Two-Color Cardigan
100

Classic Cabled Mittens
108

Classic Shrug
114

Classic Cabled Scarf
118

Waistcoat
122

INTRODUCTION

I love cables. This life-long affair began when I learned to cable knit at the age of twelve. I was completely fascinated by making twists and turns going in all directions in the knitted fabric. I never thought that several years later I would find myself designing my own cables and using traditional ones to design the garments in this book.

Cables look more difficult than they actually are. To knit a cable you simply slip stitches onto a cable needle, hold them at the front or back of the work, knit or purl stitches from the left-hand needle, then work the stitches off the cable needle. It's as simple as that! You will find a wide range of modern and fresh knitting ideas in this book. And you can rest assured that all the pattern instructions have been tried out by a professional knitter. I wish you a lot of fun knitting your favorite items from this book!

HOW TO SUBSTITUTE YARNS

Throughout this book several different brands and weights of yarn have been used. It is extremely simple to find a substitute yarn by using this simple math equation. If the garment you are going to knit takes 7 x 3.5oz/100g balls of yarn, which has a yardage of 322yds/295m and your new substitute yarn has a yardage of 197yds, you will need to divide the recommended yarn length total by the new yarn length of 197 to get the number of balls required.

For example: 7 x 322yds = 2,254yds needed (recommended). 2,254yds divided by the new yardage, which is 197yds = 11.44, so you will need 12 x 3.5oz (100g) balls to complete your garment using the new yarn. I recommend always substituting with the same or a similar weight yarn, otherwise you might encounter problems. Always knit a gauge swatch in the new yarn to match the stated gauge in the pattern.

AMOUNT OF YARN

Yarn amounts specified in the patterns can never be absolutely correct. This is partly due to the fact that tensions vary according to the knitter, but mostly because the number of yards/meters per ounce/gram varies with every color of yarn. To ensure that you will not run out of yarn, the yarn amounts given in the patterns are generous.

EQUIPMENT

Sewing needle: Always use a wool (knitter's) sewing needle for sewing, as these tend to be blunt and will not split the yarn fiber or stitches, making a neater seam.

Stitch holders: These prevent stitches from unraveling when not in use. Alternately, a spare knitting needle of the same size or less (ideally a double-pointed needle) can be used as a stitch holder. For holding just a few stitches, a safety pin is always useful.

Cable needle: There are two types of cable needles, one with a kink and the other one is straight, similar to a double-pointed needle. I recommend the one with the kink as this keeps the stitches from sliding off the needle.

GAUGE

It is important to check your gauge before you start knitting. Knit a swatch using the specified yarn and knitting needles. If there are too many stitches to your 4in/10cm sample, your tension is tight and you should change to a larger-sized needle. If there are too few stitches, your tension is loose and you should change to a smaller-sized needle.

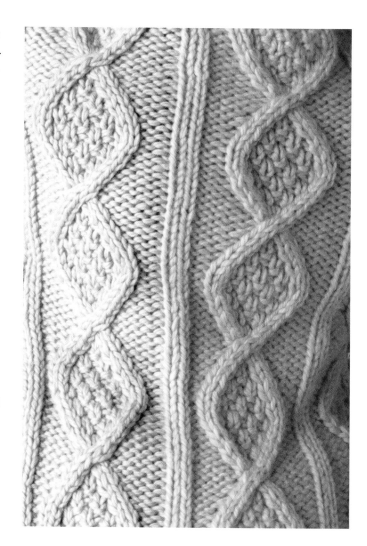

CASTING ON (Cable Method)

Although there are many different techniques for casting on stitches, the following method creates a firm and attractive edge:

First make a slip knot in the yarn and place the loop on the left-hand needle. Insert the point of the right-hand needle into the loop on the left-hand needle, wrap the yarn around the right-hand needle and draw the yarn through the loop. Pass the new loop onto the left-hand needle and pull the yarn to tighten the new loop.

Next insert the right-hand needle between the two loops on the left-hand needle, wrap the yarn around the right-hand needle and draw the yarn through. Slip the new loop onto the left-hand needle as before.

Continue in this way, inserting the needle between two loops on the left-hand needle, until you have the required number of stitches.

BASIC STITCHES

Here is how to work the simple stitches used for the patterns:

Stockinette Stitch: Alternate one row knit and one row purl. The knit side is the right side of the work unless otherwise stated in the instructions.

Garter Stitch: Knit every row. Both sides are the same and look identical.

K1, P1 Rib: Alternate one knit stitch with one purl stitch to the end of the row. On the next row, knit all the knit stitches and purl all the purl stitches as they face you.

Seed Stitch: Alternate one knit stitch with one purl stitch to the end of the row. On the next row, knit all the purl stitches and purl all the knit stitches as they face you.

JOINING YARN

Always join yarn at the beginning of a new row (unless you are working the Fair Isle or Intarsia method) and never knot the yarn as the knot may come through to the right side and spoil your work. Any long loose ends will be useful for sewing up afterward.

WORKING STRIPES

When knitting different-colored stripes, carry yarns loosely up the side of your work.

WORKING FROM A CHART

Each square on a chart represents a stitch and each line of squares a row of knitting. Alongside the chart there will be a stitch key. When working from the charts, read odd rows (knit) from right to left and even rows (purl) from left to right, unless otherwise stated.

SEAMS

I recommend using the mattress stitch as this helps matching row for row and stripe for stripe on knitted fabric. If you are unable to work the mattress stitch, then a simple backstitch will be fine. Whichever method you choose for sewing your garment together, a one stitch seam allowance has been given on all pieces.

INSTRUCTIONS IN SQUARE BRACKETS

These are to be repeated the number of times stated after the closing bracket.

NUMBERS IN PARENTHESES

The smallest size is always the first set of numbers just before the opening parenthesis with the larger sizes inside before the closing of the parenthesis. Where there is only one number without parentheses, this is for all sizes.

BINDING OFF

Always bind off as if to knit unless otherwise stated.

WORKING IN STOCKINETTE STITCH

Always begin with a Knit row unless otherwise stated.

GARTER AND CABLE SWEATER

Skill Level ★

MEASUREMENTS AND YARN

	32–34 81.5–86.5	36–38 91.5–96.5	40–42 101.5–106.5	44–46 112–117	in cm
To fit bust					
Actual size	36¾ 93.5	41¼ 105	45 114	49¾ 126.5	in cm
Full Length (approximately)	25¼ 64	26 66	28½ 72.5	29½ 75	in cm
Sleeve Length (adjustable)	18 45.5	19 48	19¾ 50	20½ 52	in cm
Plymouth Yarn® Company Homestead (100% wool) in #23 Dusty Blue	7	8	9	10	3½oz/100g 191yds/175m balls

OTHER MATERIALS

• 1 pair US 6 (4mm) knitting needles OR SIZE TO OBTAIN GAUGE

• 1 pair US 8 (5mm) knitting needles OR SIZE TO OBTAIN GAUGE

• Cable needle

• Stitch holders

Gauge: 17 sts and 36 rows = 4in/10cm in Gst using US 8 (5mm) needles.

TAKE TIME TO CHECK GAUGE.

SPECIAL ABBREVIATIONS

C6B: Slip next 3 sts onto a cable needle and hold at back, K3, then K3 from cable needle.

C6F: Slip next 3 sts onto a cable needle and hold at front, K3, then K3 from cable needle.

C5BP: Slip next 2 sts onto a cable needle and hold at back, K3, then P2 from cable needle.

C5FP: Slip next 3 sts onto a cable needle and hold at front, P2, then K3 from cable needle.

SWEATER

BACK

Using larger needles, cast on 80 (90, 98, 108) sts.

Row 1 (RS): K23 (28, 32, 37), work Row 1 of chart over next 34 sts, K23 (28, 32, 37).

Row 2: K23 (28, 32, 37), work Row 2 of chart over next 34 sts, K23 (28, 32, 37).

The last 2 rows set position of cable panel and Gst sections.

Work even as set, working appropriate row of chart until back measures 17¾ (17¾, 18½, 18½)in/45 (45, 47, 47)cm, ending with RS facing for next row.

Shape armholes

Keeping patt correct, dec 1 st at each end of every row 8 (8, 10, 10) times—64 (74, 78, 88) sts. **

Work even until armhole measures 7½ (8¼, 10, 11)in/19 (21, 25, 28)cm, ending with RS facing for next row.

Shape shoulders

Keeping patt correct, bind off 6 (9, 8, 10) sts at beg of next 2 rows, then 7 (9, 9, 11) sts at beg of foll 2 rows—38 (38, 44, 46) sts.

Bind off rem sts.

FRONT

Work as for back to **—64 (74, 78, 88) sts.

Work even in patt until armhole measures 5½ (6½, 8, 9)in/14 (16.5, 20.5, 23)cm, ending with RS facing for next row.

Shape neck

Next row (RS): Work 24 (29, 30, 34) sts in patt, place rem 40 (45, 48, 54) sts on a st holder. Turn.

Work each side of neck separately.

Next row: Bind off 3 (3, 4, 4) sts, work patt to end—21 (26, 26, 30) sts.

Next row: Work in patt to last 2 sts, patt2tog—20 (25, 25, 29) sts.

Next row: Bind off 3 (3, 4, 4) sts, work patt to end—17 (22, 21, 25) sts.

Next row: Work in patt to last 2 sts, patt2tog—16 (21, 20, 24) sts.

Next row: Bind off 3 sts, work in patt to end—13 (18, 17, 21) sts.

Work even until armhole measures same as back to start of shoulder shaping, ending with RS facing for next row.

Shape shoulder

Keeping patt correct, bind off 6 (9, 8, 10) sts at beg of next row and 7 (9, 9, 11) sts at beg of foll RS row.

To work the second side of neck, place the 40 (45, 48, 54) sts on the holder on a needle. With RS facing, rejoin yarn and bind off center 16 (16, 18, 20) sts, work in patt to end—24 (29, 30, 34) sts.

Next row (WS): Work in patt across row.

Next row: Bind off 3 (3, 4, 4) sts, work in patt to end—21 (26, 26, 30) sts.

Next row: Work in patt to last 2 sts, patt2tog—20 (25, 25, 29) sts.

Next row: Bind off 3 (3, 4, 4) sts, work in patt to end—17 (22, 21, 25) sts.

Next row: Work in patt to last 2 sts, patt2tog—16 (21, 20, 24) sts.

Next row: Bind off 3 sts, work in patt to end—13 (18, 17, 21) sts.

Work even until armhole measures same as back to start of shoulder shaping, ending with WS facing for next row.

Shape shoulder

Keeping patt correct, bind off 6 (9, 8, 10) sts at beg of next row and 7 (9, 9, 11) sts at beg of foll WS row.

SLEEVES (Make 2)

Using larger needles cast on 41 (45, 49, 53) sts.

Work in Gst throughout, inc 1 st at each end of 13th row, then every 15th row until there are 59 (63, 69, 75) sts.

Work even until sleeve measures 18 (19, 19¾, 20½)in/45.5 (48, 50, 52)cm, ending with RS facing for next row.

Shape sleeve top

Dec 1 st at each end of every row 8 (8, 10, 10) times—43 (47, 49, 55) sts.

Dec 1 st at each end of next row, then every other row 3 (1, 1, 1) times—35 (43, 45, 51) sts.

Work 1 row even in pattern.

Dec 1 st at each end of every row 10 (14, 14, 14) times—15 (15, 17, 23) sts.

Bind off rem 15 (15, 17, 23) sts.

NECKBAND

Join right shoulder.

Using smaller needles and RS facing, pick up and K23 (23, 26, 26) sts evenly down left side of neck, 16 (16, 18, 20) sts across bound-off sts at center front of neck, 23 (23, 26, 26) sts evenly up right side of neck and 38 (38, 44, 46) sts across bound-off sts at center back neck—100 (100, 114, 118) sts.

Work in Gst for 2½in/6.5cm, ending with WS facing for next row.

Bind off loosely as if to knit on WS.

FINISHING

Join left shoulder seam and neckband seam. Join side and sleeve seams. Sew sleeve tops into armholes, matching the dec rows, easing to fit.

KEY

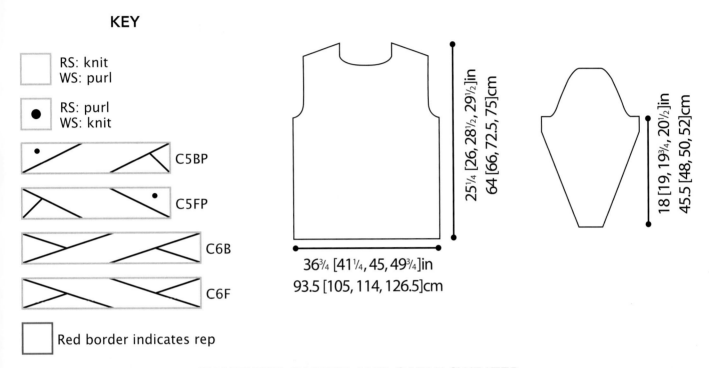

	RS: knit WS: purl
•	RS: purl WS: knit
	C5BP
	C5FP
	C6B
	C6F
	Red border indicates rep

25¼ [26, 28½, 29½]in
64 [66, 72.5, 75]cm

36¾ [41¼, 45, 49¾]in
93.5 [105, 114, 126.5]cm

18 [19, 19¾, 20½]in
45.5 [48, 50, 52]cm

CHART FOR GARTER AND CABLE SWEATER

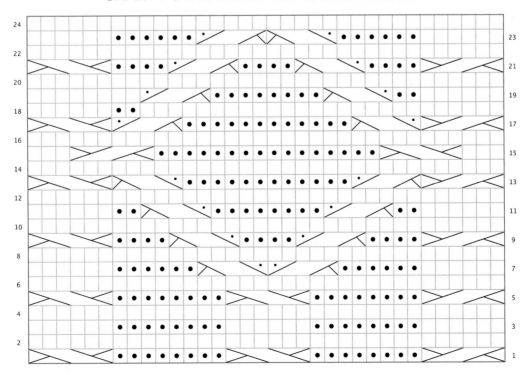

MOCK TURTLENECK PULLOVER

Skill Level ★★★

MEASUREMENTS AND YARN

	32 81.5	34 86.5	36 91.5	38 96.5	40 101.5	42 106.5	in cm
To fit bust	32 81.5	34 86.5	36 91.5	38 96.5	40 101.5	42 106.5	in cm
Actual size	34½ 87.5	37 94	39 99	41½ 105.5	43½ 110.5	45½ 115.5	in cm
Full Length (approximately)	22½ 57	23 58.5	23½ 59.5	24 61	24¼ 61.5	24½ 62	in cm
Sleeve Length (adjustable)	17½ 44.5	17½ 44.5	17½ 44.5	18 45.5	18 45.5	18 45.5	in cm
Plymouth Yarn® DK Merino Superwash (100% merino superwash wool) in #1135 Bordeaux	14	15	16	17	18	19	1¾oz/50g 130yds/119m balls

OTHER MATERIALS

• 1 pair US 3 (3.25mm) knitting needles OR SIZE TO OBTAIN GAUGE

• 1 pair US 6 (4mm) knitting needles OR SIZE TO OBTAIN GAUGE

• Cable needle

Gauge: 22 sts and 38 rows = 4in/10cm over seed st using US 6 (4mm) needles.

TAKE TIME TO CHECK GAUGE.

SPECIAL ABBREVIATIONS

W3: Wrap next 3 sts as follows: yo to make a st, K3 sts, then slip the yo over the 3 sts just knitted.

C3BP: Slip next st onto a cable needle and hold at back, K2, then P1 from cable needle.

C3FP: Slip next 2 sts onto a cable needle and hold at front, P1, then K2 from cable needle.

C4B: Slip next 2 sts onto a cable needle and hold at back, K2, then K2 from cable needle.

C4F: Slip next 2 sts onto a cable needle and hold at front, K2, then K2 from cable needle.

C4BP: Slip next st onto a cable needle and hold at back, K3, then P1 from cable needle.

C4FP: Slip next 3 sts onto a cable needle and hold at front, P1, then K3 from cable needle.

C5BP: Slip next 2 sts onto a cable needle and hold at back, K3, then P2 from cable needle.

C5FP: Slip next 3 sts onto a cable needle and hold at front, P2, then K3 from cable needle.

C6B: Slip next 3 sts onto a cable needle and hold at back, K3, then K3 from cable needle.

C6F: Slip next 3 sts onto a cable needle and hold at front, K3, then K3 from cable needle.

CL6: Slip next 6 sts onto a cable needle and hold at front, wrap yarn counterclockwise 3 times around sts on cable needle, then K6 from cable needle.

PULLOVER

BACK

Using smaller needles, cast on 96 (102, 108, 114, 120, 126) sts.

Row 1 (RS): P1 (0, 0, 0, 1, 0), K2 (2, 1, 0, 2, 2), *P2, K2, rep from * to last 1 (0, 3, 2, 1, 0) sts, P1 (0, 2, 2, 1, 0), K0 (0, 1, 0, 0, 0).

Row 2: K1 (0, 0, 0, 1, 0), P2 (2, 1, 0, 2, 2), *K2, P2, rep from * to last 1 (0, 3, 2, 1, 0) sts, K1 (0, 2, 2, 1, 0), P0 (0, 1, 0, 0, 0).

These 2 rows form ribbing.

Work in ribbing for 17 more rows, ending with WS facing for next row.

Row 20 (WS): Rib 14 (17, 20, 23, 26, 29), m1, [rib 1, m1, rib 2, m1] twice, [rib 1, m1, rib 1, m1, rib 2, m1] twice, [rib 1, m1] 3 times, rib 2, [m1, rib 1] 3 times, [m1, rib 2, m1, rib 1, m1, rib 1] twice, m1, [rib 2, m1, rib 1, m1] twice, [rib 2, m1, rib 1, m1, rib 1, m1] 3 times, rib 1, m1, rib 2, [m1, rib 1] 3 times, [m1, rib 2, m1, rib 1, m1, rib 1] twice, [m1, rib 2, m1, rib 1] twice, m1, rib to end—148 (154, 160, 166, 172, 178) sts.

Change to larger needles and patt as foll:

Row 1 (RS): K0 (1, 0, 1, 0, 1), [P1, K1] 7 (8, 10, 11, 13, 14) times, K8, [work Row 1 of Cable Panel chart over next 48 sts, K8] twice, [K1, P1] 7 (8, 10, 11, 13, 14) times, K0 (1, 0, 1, 0, 1).

Row 2: K0 (1, 0, 1, 0, 1), [P1, K1] 7 (8, 10, 11, 13, 14) times, P8, [work Row 2 of Cable Panel chart over next 48 sts, P8] twice, [K1, P1] 7 (8, 10, 11, 13, 14) times, K0 (1, 0, 1, 0, 1).

Row 3: K0 (1, 0, 1, 0, 1), [P1, K1] 7 (8, 10, 11, 13, 14) times, C4B, C4F, [work Row 3 of Cable Panel chart over next 48 sts, C4B, C4F] twice, [K1, P1] 7 (8, 10, 11, 13, 14) times, K0 (1, 0, 1, 0, 1).

Row 4: K0 (1, 0, 1, 0, 1), [P1, K1] 7 (8, 10, 11, 13, 14) times, P8, [work Row 4 of Cable Panel chart over next 48 sts, P8] twice, [K1, P1] 7 (8, 10, 11, 13, 14) times, K0 (1, 0, 1, 0, 1).

These 4 rows form patt.

Work in patt as set, working appropriate rows of Cable Panel chart, dec 1 st at each end of 9th, then every 8th row until there are 142 (148, 154, 160, 166, 172) sts, then every 6th row until there are 138 (144, 150, 156, 162, 168) sts rem.

Work 9 rows even, ending with RS facing for next row.

Inc 1 st at each end of next and every 8th row until there are 148 (154, 160, 166, 172, 178) sts, working extra sts into seed st.

Work even until back measures 14½ (15, 15, 15½, 15½, 15¾)in/37 (38, 38, 39.5, 39.5, 40cm), ending with RS facing for next row.

Shape armholes

Keeping patt correct, bind off 5 (6, 6, 7, 7, 8) sts at beg of next 2 rows—138 (142, 148, 152, 158, 162) sts.

Dec 1 st at each end of every row 3 (3, 5, 5, 7, 7) times, every other row 2 (3, 3, 4, 4, 5) times, then every 4th row until 124 (126, 128, 130, 132, 134) sts rem.

Work even until armhole measures 8 (8, 8½, 8½, 8¾, 8¾)in/20.5 (20.5, 21.5, 21.5, 22, 22)cm, ending with RS facing for next row.

Shape shoulders and back neck

Keeping patt correct, bind off 11 (11, 11, 11, 11, 12) sts at beg of next 2 rows—102 (104, 106, 108, 110, 110) sts.

Next row (RS): Bind off 11 sts, work in patt until there are 14 (14, 15, 15, 16, 16) sts on right needle, turn and work this side first.

Bind off 4 sts at beg of next row.

Bind off rem 10 (10, 11, 11, 12, 12) sts.

With RS facing, rejoin yarn to rem sts, bind off center 52 (54, 54, 56, 56, 56) sts. AT THE SAME TIME dec 24 sts evenly spaced across as you bind off. Work in patt to end. Work to match first side, reversing shapings.

FRONT

Work as for back until 18 (18, 18, 20, 20, 20) rows less than back to start of shoulder shaping, ending with RS facing for next row.

Shape neck

Next row (RS): Work 46 (46, 47, 48, 49, 50) sts in patt, turn and work this side first.

Bind off 5 sts at beg of next row—41 (41, 42, 43, 44, 45) sts.

Dec 1 st at neck edge every row 5 times, every other row 3 (3, 3, 4, 4, 4) times, then on foll 4th row—32 (32, 33, 33, 34, 35) sts.

Work 1 row, ending with RS facing for next row.

Shape shoulder

Keeping patt correct, bind off 11 (11, 11, 11, 11, 12) sts at beg of next and foll RS row.

Work 1 row.

Bind off rem 10 (10, 11, 11, 12, 11) sts.

With RS facing, rejoin yarn to rem sts, bind off center 32 (34, 34, 34, 34, 34) sts. AT THE SAME TIME dec 14 sts evenly spaced across as you bind off. Work in patt to end.

Work to match first side, reversing shapings, working an extra row before start of shoulder shaping.

SLEEVES (Make 2)

Using smaller needles cast on 50 (50, 52, 54, 54, 56) sts.

Row 1 (RS): P2 (2, 1, 2, 2, 1), K2, *P2, K2, rep from * to last 2 (2, 1, 2, 2, 1) sts, P2 (2, 1, 2, 2, 1).

Row 2: K2 (2, 1, 2, 2, 1), P2, *K2, P2, rep from * to last 2 (2, 1, 2, 2, 1) sts, K2 (2, 1, 2, 2, 1).

These 2 rows form ribbing.

Work in ribbing for 17 more rows, ending with WS facing for next row.

Row 20 (WS): Rib 20 (20, 21, 22, 22, 23), [m1, rib 1] 5 times, [rib 1, m1] 5 times, work in ribbing to end—60 (60, 62, 64, 64, 66) sts.

Change to larger needles and patt as foll;

Row 1 (RS): Inc in first st, K0 (0, 1, 0, 0, 1), [P1, K1] 10 (10, 10, 11, 11, 11) times, K8, P2, K8, [K1, P1] 10 (10, 10, 11, 11, 11) times, K0 (0, 1, 0, 0, 1), inc in last st—62 (62, 64, 66, 66, 68) sts.

Row 2: K0 (0, 1, 0, 0, 1), [P1, K1] 11 (11, 11, 12, 12, 12) times, P8, K2, P8, [K1, P1] 11 (11, 11, 12, 12, 12) times, K0 (0, 1, 0, 0, 1).

Row 3: K0 (0, 1, 0, 0, 1), [P1, K1] 11 (11, 11, 12, 12, 12) times, C4B, C4F, P2, C4B, C4F, [K1, P1] 11 (11, 11, 12, 12, 12) times, K0 (0, 1, 0, 0, 1).

Row 4: K0 (0, 1, 0, 0, 1), [P1, K1] 11 (11, 11, 12, 12, 12) times, P8, K2, P8, [K1, P1] 11 (11, 11, 12, 12, 12) times, K0 (0, 1, 0, 0, 1).

These 4 rows form patt and start sleeve shaping.

Work in patt, shaping sides by inc 1 st at each end of 5th and every 10th (8th, 8th, 8th, 8th, 8th) row until there are 82 (74, 74, 76, 86, 84) sts, working extra sts in seed st.

2nd, 3rd, 4th, 5th and 6th sizes only

Inc 1 st at each end of every 10th row until there are (84, 86, 88, 90, 92) sts.

All sizes

Work even until sleeve measures 17½ (17½, 17½, 18, 18, 18)in/44.5 (44.5, 44.5, 45.5, 45.5, 45.5)cm, ending with RS facing for next row.

Shape top

Keeping patt correct, bind off 5 (6, 6, 7, 7, 8) sts at beg of next 2 rows—72 (72, 74, 74, 76, 76) sts.

Dec 1 st at each end of every row 3 times, every other row 3 times, then every 4th row until 50 (50, 52, 52, 54, 54) sts rem.

Work 1 row, ending with RS facing for next row.

Dec 1 st at each end of next and every other row until 38 sts rem, then on every row 3 times, ending with RS facing for next row.

Bind off rem 32 sts dec 10 sts evenly across as you bind off.

FINISHING

Join right shoulder seam.

NECK BORDER

With RS facing and smaller needles, pick up and K23 (23, 23, 26, 26, 26) sts down left side of neck, 18 (20, 20, 20, 20, 20) sts from front, 23 (23, 23, 26, 26, 26) sts up right side of neck, then 34 (36, 36, 38, 38, 38) sts from back—98 (102, 102, 110, 110, 110) sts.

Row 1: P2, *K2, P2, rep from * to end.

Row 2: K2, *P2, K2, rep from * to end.

Rep the last 2 rows until neck border measures 2½in/6.5cm, ending with RS facing for next row.

Bind off in ribbing.

Join left shoulder and neck border seam. Join side and sleeve seams. Insert sleeves.

KEY

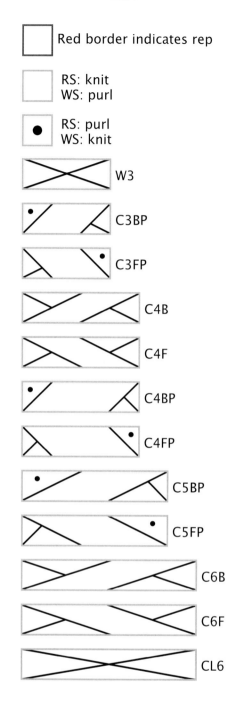

□ Red border indicates rep

□ RS: knit
WS: purl

● RS: purl
WS: knit

W3

C3BP

C3FP

C4B

C4F

C4BP

C4FP

C5BP

C5FP

C6B

C6F

CL6

34½ [37, 39, 41½, 43½, 45½]in
87.5 [94, 99, 105.5, 110.5, 115.5]cm

22½ [23, 23½, 24, 24¼, 24½]in
57 [58.5, 59.5, 61, 61.5, 62]cm

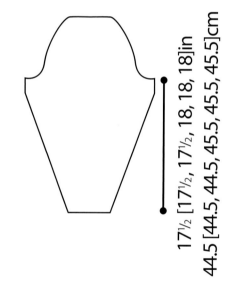

17½ [17½, 17½, 18, 18, 18]in
44.5 [44.5, 44.5, 45.5, 45.5, 45.5]cm

MOCK TURTLENECK PULLOVER CHART

CARDIGAN

BACK

Using smaller needles and yarn A, cast on 82 (90, 98, 110, 118, 130) sts.

Row 1 (RS): K2, *P2, K2, rep from * to end.

Row 2: P2, *K2, P2, rep from * to end.

The last 2 rows form ribbing.

Work 4 more rows in ribbing, dec 1 (1, 0, 1, 0, 1) st at each end of last row and ending with RS facing for next row—80 (88, 98, 108, 118, 128) sts.

Change to larger needles.

Row 1 (RS): K0 (4, 3, 2, 1, 0), P2, *K4, P2, rep from * to last 0 (4, 3, 2, 1, 0) sts, K0 (4, 3, 2, 1, 0).

Row 2: P0 (4, 3, 2, 1, 0), K2, *P4, K2, rep from * to last 0 (4, 3, 2, 1, 0) sts, P0 (4, 3, 2, 1, 0).

Row 3: K0 (4, 3, 2, 1, 0), P2, *C4F, P2, rep from * to last 0 (4, 3, 2, 1, 0) sts, K0 (4, 3, 2, 1, 0).

Row 4: P0 (4, 3, 2, 1, 0), K2, *P4, K2, rep from * to last 0 (4, 3, 2, 1, 0) sts, P0 (4, 3, 2, 1, 0).

The last 4 rows form patt.

Work even in patt until back measures 7½ (8, 8½, 8¾, 9, 9½)in/19 (20.5, 21.5, 22, 23, 24)cm, ending with RS facing for next row.

Shape armhole

Keeping patt correct, bind off 6 (7, 8, 9, 10, 12) sts at beg of next 2 rows—68 (74, 82, 90, 98, 104) sts.

Dec 1 st at each end of next 5 (5, 7, 9, 11, 11) then every other row 2 times—54 (60, 64, 68, 72, 78) sts.

Work even until armhole measures 8 (8½, 8¾, 9, 9½, 10) in/20.5 (21.5, 22, 23, 24, 25.5)cm, ending with RS facing for next row.

Shape shoulders and back neck

Keeping patt correct, bind off 7 (8, 9, 10, 11, 12) sts, patt until there are 11 (12, 13, 13, 14, 15) sts on right-hand needle, place rem sts on a st holder. Turn.

Work each side of neck separately.

Bind off 3 sts at beg of next row.

Bind off rem 8 (9, 10, 10, 11, 12) sts.

Leave center 18 (20, 20, 22, 22, 24) sts on holder. With RS facing, place rem sts on needle, rejoin yarn and work in patt to end. Complete to match first side, reversing shapings.

LEFT FRONT

Using smaller needles and yarn A, cast on 39 (43, 47, 51, 57, 61) sts.

Row 1 (RS): P0 (0, 0, 0, 2, 2), *K2, P2, rep from * to last 3 sts, K2, P1.

Row 2: K1, P2, *K2, P2, rep from * to last 0 (0, 0, 0, 2, 2) sts , K0 (0, 0, 0, 2, 2).

The last 2 rows form ribbing.

Work 4 more rows in ribbing, dec (dec, –, inc, –, inc) 1 st at end of last row and ending with RS facing for next row—38 (42, 47, 52, 57, 62) sts.

Change to larger needles.

Row 1 (RS): K0 (4, 3, 2, 1, 0), P2, *K4, P2, rep from * to end.

Row 2: K2, *P4, K2, rep from * to last 0 (4, 3, 2, 1, 0) sts, P0 (4, 3, 2, 1, 0).

Row 3: K0 (4, 3, 2, 1, 0), P2, *C4F, P2, rep from * to end.

Row 4: K2, *P4, K2, rep from * to last 0 (4, 3, 2, 1, 0) sts, P0 (4, 3, 2, 1, 0).

The last 4 rows form patt.

Work even until left front measures 6 rows less than back to start of armhole shaping, ending with RS facing for next row.

Shape front slope

Keeping patt correct, dec 1 st at end of next and foll 4th row—36 (40, 45, 50, 55, 60) sts.

Work 1 row in patt, ending with RS facing for next row.

Shape armhole

Keeping patt correct, bind off 6 (7, 8, 9, 10, 12) sts at beg of next row—30 (33, 37, 41, 45, 48) sts.

Work 1 row in patt, ending with RS facing for next row.

Dec 1 st at armhole edge on next 5 (5, 7, 9, 11, 11) rows, then on every other row 2 times, AT THE SAME TIME, dec 1 st at neck edge on next row, then every 4th row 3 (3, 3, 4, 4, 4) times—19 (22, 24, 25, 27, 30) sts.

Dec 1 st at neck edge only on 4th (4th, 2nd, 4th, 4th, 2nd) row, then on every 4th row 0 (2, 1, 2, 2, 3) times, then on every 6th row 3 (2, 3, 2, 2, 2) times—15 (17, 19, 20, 22, 24) sts.

Work even until left front matches back to start of shoulder shaping, ending with RS facing for next row.

Shape shoulder

Keeping patt correct, bind off 7 (8, 9, 10, 11, 12) sts at beg of next row.

Work 1 row in patt.

Bind off rem 8 (9, 10, 10, 11, 12) sts.

RIGHT FRONT

Using smaller needles and yarn A, cast on 39 (43, 47, 51, 57, 61) sts.

Row 1 (RS): P1, K2, *P2, K2, rep from * to last 0 (0, 0, 0, 2, 2) sts, P0 (0, 0, 0, 2, 2).

Row 2: K0 (0, 0, 0, 2, 2), *P2, K2, rep from * to last 3 sts, P2, K1.

The last 2 rows form ribbing.

Work 4 more rows in ribbing, dec (dec, –, inc, –, inc) 1 st at beg of last row and ending with RS facing for next row—38 (42, 47, 52, 57, 62) sts.

Change to larger needles.

Row 1 (RS): P2, *K4, P2, rep from * to last 0 (4, 3, 2, 1, 0) sts, K0 (4, 3, 2, 1, 0).

Row 2: P0 (4, 3, 2, 1, 0), K2, *P4, K2, rep from * to end.

Row 3: P2, *C4F, P2, rep from * to last 0 (4, 3, 2, 1, 0) sts, K0 (4, 3, 2, 1, 0).

Row 4: P0 (4, 3, 2, 1, 0), K2, *P4, K2, rep from * to end.

The last 4 rows form patt.

Work even until left front measures 6 rows less than back to start of armhole shaping, ending with RS facing for next row.

Shape front slope

Keeping patt correct, dec 1 st at beg of next and foll 4th row—36 (40, 45, 50, 55, 60) sts.

Work 2 rows in patt, ending with WS facing for next row.

Shape armhole

Keeping patt correct, bind off 6 (7, 8, 9, 10, 12) sts at beg of next row—30 (33, 37, 41, 45, 48) sts.

Dec 1 st at armhole edge of next 5 (5, 7, 9, 11, 11) rows, then on every other row 2 times, AT THE SAME TIME, dec 1 st at neck edge on next row, then every 4th row 3 (3, 3, 4, 4, 4) times—19 (22, 24, 25, 27, 30) sts.

Dec 1 st at neck edge only on 4th (4th, 2nd, 4th, 4th, 2nd) row, then on every 4th row 0 (2, 1, 2, 2, 3) times, then on every 6th row 3 (2, 3, 2, 2, 2) times—15 (17, 19, 20, 22, 24) sts.

Work even until left front matches back to start of shoulder shaping, ending with WS facing for next row.

Shape shoulder

Keeping patt correct, bind off 7 (8, 9, 10, 11, 12) sts at beg of next row.

Work 1 row in patt.

Bind off rem 8 (9, 10, 10, 11, 12) sts.

SLEEVES (Make 2)

Using smaller needles and yarn B, cast on 30 (34, 34, 34, 38, 38) sts.

Row 1 (RS): K2, *P2, K2, rep from * to end.

Row 2: P2, *K2, P2, rep from * to end.

The last 2 rows form ribbing.

Work 7 more rows in ribbing, ending with WS facing for next row.

Change to larger needles. Work in patt as folls:

Row 1 (WS): Using yarn B, Knit.

Row 2: Using yarn B, Purl.

Join yarn A.

Row 3: Using yarn A, P2, *sl 2 wyab, P2, rep from * to end.

Row 4: Using yarn A, K2, *sl 2 wyaf, K2, rep from * to end.

Rows 5 and 6: Rep Rows 1 and 2.

Row 7: Using yarn A, P1, sl 1 wyab, P2, *sl 2 wyab, P2, rep from * to last 2 sts, sl 1 wyab, P1.

Row 8: Using yarn A, K1, sl 1 wyaf, K2, *sl 2 wyaf, K2, rep from * to last 2 sts, sl 1 wyaf, K1.

The last 8 rows form patt.

Work even in patt as set, inc 1 st at each end of next, then on every 10th row until there are 48 (50, 52, 54, 58, 62) sts, working all inc sts in patt.

Work even until sleeve measures 17¾ (18, 18½, 18½, 18½, 19)in/ 45 (45.5, 47, 47, 47, 48)cm, ending with RS facing for next row.

Shape top

Keeping patt correct, bind off 6 (7, 8, 9, 10, 12) sts at beg of next 2 rows—36 (36, 36, 36, 38, 38) sts. Dec 1 st at each end of next 3 rows, then on every 4th row 4 (5, 6, 6, 7, 7) times, then on every other row until 6 sts rem.

Patt 1 row, ending with RS facing for next row.

Bind off rem 6 sts.

FRONT BORDER

Join both shoulder seams.

With RS facing and using circular needle and yarn A, beg and ending at cast-on edge, pick up and K26 (27, 28, 30, 32, 34) sts up right front opening to beg of front slope shaping, 37 (39, 40, 43, 43, 44) sts up right front slope, and 3 sts down right side of back neck, K across 18 (20, 20, 22, 22, 24) sts from back st holder, pick up and K3 sts up left side of back neck, 37 (39, 40, 43, 43, 44) sts down left front slope to beg of front slope shaping and 26 (27, 28, 30, 32, 34) sts down left front opening edge—150 (158, 162, 174, 178, 186) sts.

Row 1 (WS): P2, *K2, P2, rep from * to end.

Row 2: K2, *P2, K2, rep from * to end.

The last 2 rows form ribbing.

Work 1 more row in ribbing as set.

Buttonhole row (RS): Rib 2, [yo, rib2tog, rib 8 (9, 9, 10, 11, 12)] twice, yo, rib2tog, rib 2 (1, 2, 2, 2, 2).

Work 3 rows in ribbing, ending with RS facing for next row.

Bind off in ribbing.

FINISHING

Sew in sleeves. Join side and sleeve seams. Sew on buttons to correspond with buttonholes.

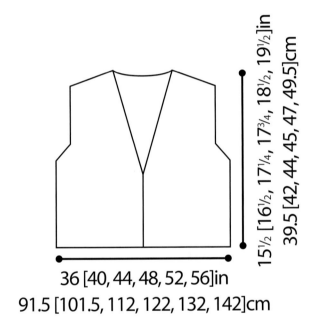

15½ [16½, 17¼, 17¾, 18½, 19½]in
39.5 [42, 44, 45, 47, 49.5]cm

36 [40, 44, 48, 52, 56]in
91.5 [101.5, 112, 122, 132, 142]cm

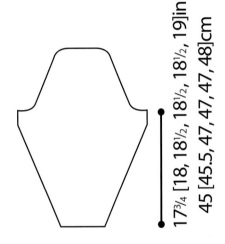

17¾ [18, 18½, 18½, 18½, 19]in
45 [45.5, 47, 47, 47, 48]cm

MEN'S TWO-COLOR PULLOVER

Skill Level ★★

MEASUREMENTS AND YARN

To fit bust	36 91.5	38 96.5	40 101.5	42 106.5	44 112	46 117	in cm
Actual size	38½ 98	40 101.5	43¾ 111	45¼ 115	47¼ 120	48¾ 124	in cm
Full Length [approximately]	27¼ 69	27¼ 69	28¼ 72	28¼ 72	29¼ 74.5	29¼ 74.5	in cm
Sleeve Length [adjustable]	17¾ 45	18 45.5	18½ 47	19¼ 49	19¼ 49	19¼ 49	in cm
Rowan Felted Tweed Aran (50% merino wool, 25% alpaca, 25% viscose) in #732 Cherry (A)	6	6	7	7	8	8	1¾oz/50g 95yds/87m balls
Rowan Felted Tweed Aran (50% merino wool, 25% alpaca, 25% viscose) in #736 Madras (B)	16	17	18	19	20	21	1¾oz/50g 95yds/87m balls

OTHER MATERIALS

- 1 pair US 6 (4mm) knitting needles OR SIZE TO OBTAIN GAUGE
- 1 pair US 8 (5mm) knitting needles OR SIZE TO OBTAIN GAUGE
- Cable needle
- Stitch holders

Gauge: 18 sts and 24 rows = 4in/10cm over double seed st using US 8 (5mm) needles.

TAKE TIME TO CHECK GAUGE.

SPECIAL ABBREVIATIONS

C2B: Slip next st onto a cable needle and hold at back, K1, then K1 from cable needle.

C2F: Slip next st onto a cable needle and hold at front, K1, then K1 from cable needle.

C4B: Slip next 2 sts onto a cable needle and hold at back, K2, then K2 from cable needle.

C4F: Slip next 2 sts onto a cable needle and hold at front, K2, then K2 from cable needle.

T6B: Slip next 4 sts onto a cable needle and hold at back, K2, then slip the 2 purl sts from cable needle back onto left-hand needle and purl them, then K2 from cable needle.

T6F: Slip next 4 sts onto a cable needle and hold at front, K2, then slip the 2 purl sts from cable needle back onto left-hand needle and purl them, then K2 from cable needle.

M3: Make 3 sts out of 1 st by working into front, back, and front of same st.

PULLOVER

BACK

Using smaller needles and yarn A, cast on 86 (90, 98, 102, 106, 110) sts.

Row 1 [RS]: K2, *P2, K2, rep from * to end.

Row 2: P2, *K2, P2, rep from * to end.

The last 2 rows form ribbing.

Change to yarn B and work 13 (13, 13, 15, 15, 15) more rows in ribbing as set, ending with WS facing for next row.

Next row [WS]: Rib 6 (8, 5, 7, 1, 3), [m1, rib 3, m1, rib 2 (2, 3, 3, 4, 4)] to last 5 (7, 3, 5, 0, 2) sts, rib 5 (7, 3, 5, 0, 2)—116 (120, 128, 132, 136, 140) sts.

Change to larger needles.

Row 1 [RS]: P1, [K1, P1] 4 (5, 7, 8, 9, 10) times, P1, C2B, P14, work Row 1 of chart over next 64 sts, P14, C2F, P1, [P1, K1] 4 (5, 7, 8, 9, 10), P1 times.

Row 2: K1, [P1, K1] 4 (5, 7, 8, 9, 10) times, K1, P2, K1, [P3tog, m3] 3 times, K1, work Row 2 of chart over next 64 sts, K1, [m3, P3tog] 3 times, K1, P2, K1, [K1, P1] 4 (5, 7, 8, 9, 10) times, K1.

Row 3: K1, [P1, K1] 4 (5, 7, 8, 9, 10) times, P1, C2B, P14, work Row 3 of chart over next 64 sts, P14, C2F, P1, [K1, P1] 4 (5, 7, 8, 9, 10) times, K1.

Row 4: P1, [K1, P1] 4 (5, 7, 8, 9, 10) times, K1, P2, K1, [m3, P3tog] 3 times, K1, work Row 4 of chart over next 64 sts, K1, [P3tog, m3] 3 times, K1, P2, K1, [P1, K1] 4 (5, 7, 8, 9, 10) times, P1.

The last 4 rows position chart with double seed st on either side.

Work even as set, working appropriate row of chart until back measures 17½ (17, 17½, 17, 17½, 17)in/44.5 (43, 44.5, 43, 44.5, 43)cm, ending with RS facing for next row.

Change to yarn A and cont as set until back measures 18 (17¾, 18, 17¾, 18, 17¾)in/45.5 (45, 45.5, 45, 45.5, 45) cm, ending with RS facing for next row.

Shape raglans

Keeping patt correct, bind off 4 (4, 5, 5, 6, 6) sts at beg of next 2 rows—108 (112, 118, 122, 124, 128) sts.

Next row [RS]: K2, skpo, work in patt to last 4 sts, K2tog, K2.

Next row: P3, work in patt to last 3 sts, P3.

The last 2 rows set raglan shaping.

Rep the last 2 rows 11 (12, 14, 15, 19, 20) times more—84 (86, 88, 90, 84, 86) sts.

Next row [RS]: K2, skpo, work in patt to last 4 sts, K2tog, k2.

Next row: P2, P2tog, work in patt to last 4 sts, P2tog tbl, P2.

The last 2 rows set raglan shaping. **

Rep the last 2 rows 12 (12, 12, 12, 10, 10) times more—32 (34, 36, 38, 40, 42) sts.

Place rem 32 (34, 36, 38, 40, 42) sts on a st holder.

FRONT

Work as given for back to **—80 (82, 84, 86, 80, 82) sts.

Next row [RS]: K2, skpo, work in patt to last 4 sts, K2tog, K2.

Next row: P2, P2tog, work in patt to last 4 sts, P2tog tbl, P2.

The last 2 rows set raglan shaping.

Rep the last 2 rows 7 (7, 7, 7, 5, 5) times more—48 (50, 52, 54, 56, 58) sts.

Shape neck

Next row [RS]: K2, skpo, work 10 sts in patt, turn. Place rem 34 (36, 38, 40, 42, 44) sts on a st holder.

Working on these 13 sts only proceed as folls:

Next row [WS]: Work in patt to last 4 sts, P2tog tbl, P2.

Work 4 rows, dec 1 st at raglan edge as before on every row and AT THE SAME TIME dec 1 st at neck edge on every row—4 sts.

Next row [RS]: K1, sl1, K2tog, psso—2 sts.

Next row: P2tog. Fasten off.

Leaving center 20 (22, 24, 26, 28, 30) sts from back neck on holder, place rem 14 sts on needle with RS facing. Rejoin yarn B to rem 14 sts and work patt to last 4 sts, K2tog, K2—13 sts.

Next row [WS]: P2, P2tog, work in patt to end—12 sts.

Work 4 rows, dec 1 st at neck edge and AT THE SAME TIME dec 1 st at raglan edge as before on every row—4 sts.

Next row [RS]: K3tog, K1—2 sts.

Next row: P2tog. Fasten off.

SLEEVES (Make 2)

Using smaller needles and yarn A, cast on 38 (38, 42, 42, 46, 46) sts.

Row 1 [RS]: K2, *P2, K2, rep from * to end.

Row 2: P2, *K2, P2, rep from * to end.

The last 2 rows form ribbing.

Change to yarn B and work 13 (13, 13, 15, 15, 15) more rows in ribbing as set, ending with WS facing for next row.

Next row [WS]: Rib 3 (3, 5, 5, 7, 7), [m1, rib 1] to last 3 (3, 5, 5, 7, 7) sts, rib 3 (3, 5, 5, 7, 7)—70 (70, 74, 74, 78, 78) sts.

Change to larger needles.

Row 1 [RS]: [P1, K1] 1 (1, 2, 2, 3, 3) times, P1, work Row 1 of chart over next 64 sts, P1, [K1, P1] 1 (1, 2, 2, 3, 3) times.

Row 2: [K1, P1] 1 (1, 2, 2, 3, 3) times, K1, work Row 2 of chart over next 64 sts, K1, [P1, K1] 1 (1, 2, 2, 3, 3) times.

Row 3: [K1, P1] 1 (1, 2, 2, 3, 3) times, P1, work Row 3 of chart over next 64 sts, P1, [P1, K1] 1 (1, 2, 2, 3, 3) times.

Row 4: [P1, K1] 1 (1, 2, 2, 3, 3) times, K1, work Row 4 of chart over next 64 sts, K1, [K1, P1] 1 (1, 2, 2, 3, 3) times.

The last 4 rows position chart with double seed st either side.

Work in patt as set, working appropriate row of chart and AT THE SAME TIME inc 1 st at each end of next and every 8th (6th, 6th, 6th, 4th, 4th) row until there are 90 (94, 100, 104, 110, 114) sts, working extra sts in double seed st.

Work even until sleeve measures 17 (17½, 17¾, 18½, 18½, 18½)in/43 (44.5, 45, 47, 47, 47)cm, ending with RS facing for next row.

Change to yarn A and work even as set until sleeve measures 17¾ (18, 18½, 19¼, 19¼, 19¼)in/45 (45.5, 47, 49, 49, 49)cm, ending with RS facing for next row.

Shape raglans

Keeping patt correct, bind off 4 (4, 5, 5, 6, 6) sts at beg of next 2 rows—82 (86, 90, 94, 98, 102) sts.

Next row [RS]: K2, skpo, work in patt to last 4 sts, K2tog, K2.

Next row, P3, work in patt to last 3 sts, P3.

The last 2 rows set raglan shaping.

Rep the last 2 rows 22 (22, 24, 24, 26, 26) times more—36 (40, 40, 44, 44, 48) sts.

Next row [RS]: K2, skpo, work in patt to last 4 sts, K2tog, k2.

Next row: P2, P2tog, work in patt to last 4 sts, P2tog tbl, P2.

The last 2 rows set raglan shaping.

Rep the last 2 rows 1 (2, 2, 3, 3, 4) times more—28 sts.

Leave rem 28 sts on a st holder.

NECKBAND

Join raglan seams, leaving left back raglan open.

With RS facing using yarn B and smaller needles, work across the 28 sts left on st holder at top of left sleeve as follows: [K1, K2tog] 9 times, K1, pick up and K6 sts evenly along left side of neck; work across 20 (22, 24, 26, 28, 30) sts left on st holder at front of neck as follows: K1 (2, 3, 0, 1, 2), K2tog, [K2, K2tog] 4 (4, 4, 6, 6, 6) times, K1 (2, 3, 0, 1, 2); pick up and K6 sts evenly along right side of neck; work across the 28 sts left on st holder at top of right sleeve as follows: [K1, K2tog] 9 times, K1; then work across the 32 (34, 36, 38, 40, 42) sts left on st holder at back of neck as follows: K3 (4, 5, 2, 3, 4), K2tog, [K2, K2tog] 6 (6, 6, 8, 8, 8) times, K3 (4, 5, 2, 3, 4)—90 (94, 98, 98, 102, 106) sts.

Next row [WS]: P2, *K2, P2, rep from * to end.

Next row: K2, *P2, K2, rep from * to end.

The last 2 rows form ribbing.

Work 5 more rows in ribbing.

Change to yarn A and work 2 more rows.

Bind off loosely in ribbing.

FINISHING

Join left back raglan and neckband.

Join side and sleeve seams.

KEY

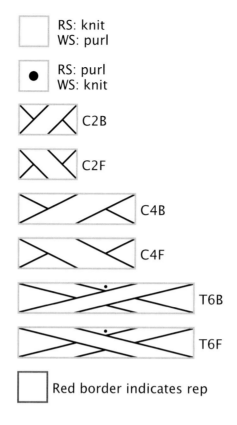

□ RS: knit
WS: purl

⬛• RS: purl
WS: knit

C2B

C2F

C4B

C4F

T6B

T6F

□ Red border indicates rep

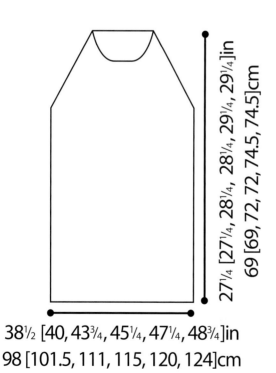

27¼ [27¼, 28¼, 28¼, 29¼, 29¼]in
69 [69, 72, 72, 74.5, 74.5]cm

38½ [40, 43¾, 45¼, 47¼, 48¾]in
98 [101.5, 111, 115, 120, 124]cm

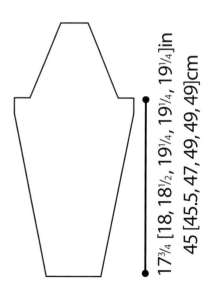

17¾ [18, 18½, 19¼, 19¼, 19¼]in
45 [45.5, 47, 49, 49, 49]cm

MEN'S TWO-COLOR PULLOVER CHART

RAPUNZEL SWEATER

Skill Level ★★★

MEASUREMENTS AND YARN

To fit bust	32–34 81.5–86.5	36–38 91.5–96.5	40–42 101.5–106.5	44–46 112–117	48–50 122–127	52–54 132–137	in cm
Actual size	36 91.5	40 101.5	44 112	48 122	52 132	56 142	in cm
Full Length (approximately)	23½ 59.5	24 61	24½ 62	25 63.5	25½ 65	26 66	in cm
Sleeve Length (adjustable)	18 45.5	18 45.5	18 45.5	18 45.5	18 45.5	18 45.5	in cm
Juniper Moon Farm Moonshine (40% wool, 40% alpaca, 20% silk) in #03 Conch Shell	8	9	10	11	12	13	3½oz/100g 197yds/180m balls

OTHER MATERIALS

• 1 pair US 5 (3.75mm) knitting needles OR SIZE TO OBTAIN GAUGE

• 1 pair US 7 (4.5mm) knitting needles OR SIZE TO OBTAIN GAUGE

• 1 set of 4 US 6 (4mm) DPNs

• Stitch holders

• Stitch markers

• 2 cable needles

• 13 buttons

Gauge: 18 sts and 31 rows = 4in/10cm in seed st using US 7 (4.5mm) needles.

TAKE TIME TO CHECK GAUGE.

SPECIAL ABBREVIATIONS

C24B: Slip next 12 sts onto a cable needle and hold at back, slip next 4 sts onto a 2nd cable needle and hold at front, K4, then K4 from 2nd cable needle, K4, slip all the sts from 1st cable needle back onto left-hand needle, slip next 4 sts onto a cable needle and hold at front, K4, then K4 from cable needle, K4.

C8B: Slip next 4 sts onto a cable needle and hold at back, K4, then K4 from cable needle.

C8F: Slip next 4 sts onto a cable needle and hold at front, K4, then K4 from cable needle.

M1 purlwise: Pick up horizontal loop lying between the st on right-hand needle and the next st on left-hand needle. Place this st onto left-hand needle and purl into the back of it.

SWEATER

FRONT

Using smaller needles, CO 130 (142, 150, 162, 170, 182) sts.

Knit 2 rows.

Change to larger needles.

Row 1 (RS): [K1, P1] 5 (7, 9, 12, 14, 17) times, pm, work Row 1 of Hip Braid chart over next 36 sts, pm, K1, [P1, K1] 2 (3, 3, 3, 3, 3) times, pm, work Row 1 of Center Braid chart over next 28 sts, pm, K1, [P1, K1] 2 (3, 3, 3, 3, 3) times, pm, work Row 1 of Hip Braid chart over next 36 sts, pm, [P1, K1] 5 (7, 9, 12, 14, 17) times—166 (178, 186, 198, 206, 218) sts.

Row 2: [K1, P1] 5 (7, 9, 12, 14, 17) times, sm, work Row 2 of Hip Braid chart over next 48 sts, sm, K1, [P1, K1] 2 (3, 3, 3, 3, 3) times, sm, work Row 2 of Center Braid chart over next 40 sts, sm, K1, [P1, K1] 2 (3, 3, 3, 3, 3) times, sm, work Row 2 of Hip Braid chart over next 48 sts, sm, [P1, K1] 5 (7, 9, 12, 14, 17) times.

The last 2 rows set the seed st and cable charts. Work even as set until the Hip Braid chart is completed, ending with RS facing for next row—126 (138, 146, 158, 166, 178) sts.

Next row (RS—braid pleat): [K1, P1] 5 (7, 9, 12, 14, 17) times, sm, P2, make pleat as follows: [slip the next 12 sts onto a cable needle and place on top of the next 12 sts on left-hand needle, with RS facing, knit through the two layers of sts by inserting the right-hand needle into the next st on the cable needle and into the next st on the left-hand needle and knitting them together forming a pleat; rep across the 12 sts], P2, sm, K1, [P1, K1] 2 (3, 3, 3, 3, 3) times, sm, work Row 41 of Center Braid chart over next 40 sts, sm, K1, [P1, K1] 2 (3, 3, 3, 3, 3) times, sm, P2, make pleat as follows: [slip the next 12 sts onto a cable needle and place behind the next 12 sts on left-hand needle, with RS facing, knit through the two layers by inserting the right-hand nee-dle into the next st on left-hand needle and into the next st on cable needle and knit them together forming a pleat; rep across the 12 sts], P2, sm, [P1, K1] 5 (7, 9, 12, 14, 17) ti-mes—102 (114, 122, 134, 142, 154) sts.

Next row: [K1, P1] 5 (7, 9, 12, 14, 17) times, sm, K2, P12, K2, sm, K1, [P1, K1] 2 (3, 3, 3, 3, 3) times, sm, work Row 42 of Center Braid chart over next 40 sts, sm, K1, [P1, K1] 2 (3, 3, 3, 3, 3) times, sm, K2, P12, K2, sm, [P1, K1] 5 (7, 9, 12, 14, 17) times.

Row 1 (RS): [K1, P1] 5 (7, 9, 12, 14, 17) times, sm, work Row 1 of Single Braid chart over next 16 sts, sm, K1, [P1, K1] 2 (3, 3, 3, 3, 3) times, sm, work Row 43 of Center Braid chart over next 40 sts, sm, K1, [P1, K1] 2 (3, 3, 3, 3, 3) times, sm, work Row 1 of Single Braid chart over next 16 sts, sm, [P1, K1] 5 (7, 9, 12, 14, 17) times.

The last row sets seed st and cable charts.

Work even as set working appropriate rows on charts until Row 60 of Center Braid chart has been worked, ending with RS facing for next row. Front should measure 8in/20.5cm.

*** Keeping patt correct, inc 1 st at each end of next row, then every 6th (6th, 6th, 6th, 6th, 8th) row 6 (5, 5, 5, 5, 4) times, then every 8th (10th, 10th, 10th, 10th, 10th) row 2 times, working all inc sts in seed st—120 (130, 138, 150, 158, 168) sts.

Work even as set working appropriate rows on charts until Row 14 of Center Braid chart has been worked, en-ding with RS facing for next row. Front should measure 15½in/39.5cm.

Armhole shaping

Keeping patt correct, bind off 3 (3, 4, 4, 5, 5) sts at the beg of the next 2 rows—114 (124, 130, 142, 148, 158) sts.

Dec 1 st at each end of next and then every other row 1 (3, 4, 5, 3, 6) times, then every 4th row 0 (0, 0, 2, 3, 3) times—110 (116, 120, 126, 134, 138) sts. ****

Work even in patt as set until armhole measures 5¾ (6¼, 6¾, 7¼, 7¾, 8¼)in/14.5 (16, 17, 18.5, 19.5, 21)cm, ending with RS facing for next row.

Neck shaping

Work 37 (40, 42, 45, 49, 51) sts in patt, place rem sts on a st holder. Turn.

Work each side of neck separately.

Keeping patt correct and working appropriate rows on Single Braid chart, dec 1 st at neck edge every row 3 (3, 5, 6, 6, 6) times, then every other row 1 (1, 1, 3, 3, 3) times—33 (36, 36, 36, 40, 42) sts.

Work even in patt as set until armhole measures 8 (8½, 9, 9½, 10, 10½)in/20.5 (21.5, 23, 24, 25.5, 26.5)cm, ending with RS facing for next row.

Shoulder

Bind off 8 (9, 9, 9, 10, 10) sts at beg of next and 2 foll RS rows, then 9 (9, 9, 9, 10, 12) sts at the beg of the foll RS row.

Leave center 36 sts on holder. With RS facing, place rem sts on needle, rejoin yarn and work in patt to end—37 (40, 42, 45, 49, 51) sts.

Complete to match first side, reversing shapings.

BACK

Left Side Back

Using smaller needles cast on 67 (73, 77, 83, 87, 93) sts.

Knit 2 rows.

Change to larger needles.

Row 1 (RS): Work Row 1 of Left Side Back cable over next 16 sts, pm, K1, [P1, K1] 2 (3, 3, 3, 3, 3) times, pm, work Row 1 of Hip Braid cable over next 36 sts, pm, [P1, K1] 5 (7, 9, 12, 14, 17) times—85 (91, 95, 101, 105, 111) sts.

Row 2: [K1, P1] 5 (7, 9, 12, 14, 17) times, sm, work Row 2 of Hip Braid cable over next 48 sts, sm, K1, [P1, K1] 2 (3, 3, 3, 3, 3) times, sm, work Row 2 Left Side Back cable over next 22 sts.

The last 2 rows set seed st, cable charts, and button placket.

Cont to work as set until the Hip Braid chart is completed, repeating Rows 3–10 on Left Side Back cable chart 4 times, then Rows 3–8 once more, ending with RS facing for next row—65 (71, 75, 81, 85, 91) sts.

Row 1 (RS—braid pleat): Work Row 9 of Left Side Back cable over next 22 sts, sm, K1, [P1, K1] 2 (3, 3, 3, 3, 3) times, sm, P2, make pleat as follows: [slip the next 12 sts onto a cable needle and place behind the next 12 sts on left-hand needle, with RS facing knit through the two layers of sts by inserting the right-hand needle into the next st on the cable needle and into the next st on the left-hand needle and knitting them together forming a pleat; rep across the 12 sts], P2, sm, [P1, K1] 5 (7, 9, 12, 14, 17) times—53 (59, 63, 69, 73, 79) sts.

Row 2: [K1, P1] 5 (7, 9, 12, 14, 17) times, sm, K2, P12, K2, sm, K1, [P1, K1] 2 (3, 3, 3, 3, 3) times, sm, work Row 10 of Left Side Back cable over next 22 sts.

Row 3: Work Row 11 of Left Side Back cable over next 22 sts, sm, K1, [P1, K1] 2 (3, 3, 3, 3, 3) times, sm, work Row 1 of Single Braid Cable over next 16 sts, sm, [P1, K1] 5 (7, 9, 12, 14, 17) times.

Row 4: [K1, P1] 5 (7, 9, 12, 14, 17) times, sm, work Row 2 of Single Braid Cable over next 16 sts, sm, K1, [P1, K1] 2 (3, 3, 3, 3, 3) times, sm, work Row 12 of Left Side Back cable over next 22 sts.

The last 2 rows set seed st, Single Braid cable, Left Side Back cable, and button placket.

Keeping pattern correct, work appropriate rows on both charts until all 24 rows of Left Side Back cable are completed, ending with RS facing for next row.

Break off yarn and place sts on a holder.

Right Side Back

Using smaller needles cast on 67 (73, 77, 83, 87, 93) sts.

Knit 2 rows.

Change to larger needles.

Row 1 (RS): [K1, P1] 5 (7, 9, 12, 14, 17) times, pm, work Row 1 of Hip Braid cable over next 36 sts, pm, K1, [P1, K1] 2 (3, 3, 3, 3, 3) times, work Row 1 of Right Side Back cable over next 16 sts—85 (91, 95, 101, 105, 111) sts.

Row 2: Work Row 2 of Right Side Back cable over next 22 sts, sm, K1, [P1, K1] 2 (3, 3, 3, 3, 3) times, sm, work Row 2 of Hip Braid cable over next 48 sts, sm, [P1, K1] 5 (7, 9, 12, 14, 17) times.

The last 2 rows set seed st, cable charts, and buttonhole placket.

Work even as set until the Hip Braid chart is completed, repeating rows 3–10 on Right Side Back cable chart 4 times, then rows 3–8 once more, ending with RS facing for next row—65 (71, 75, 81, 85, 91) sts.

Row 1 (RS—braid pleat): [K1, P1] 5 (7, 9, 12, 14, 17) times, sm, P2, make pleat as follows: [slip the next 12 sts onto a cable needle and place on top of the next 12 sts on left-hand needle, with RS facing knit through the two layers sts by inserting the right-hand needle into the next st on the cable needle and into the next st on the left-hand needle and knitting them together forming a pleat; rep across the 12 sts], P2, sm, K1, [P1, K1] 2 (3, 3, 3, 3, 3) times, sm, work Row 9 of Right Side Back cable over next 22 sts—53 (59, 63, 69, 73, 79) sts.

Row 2: Work Row 10 of Right Side Back cable over next 22 sts, sm, K1, [P1, K1] 2 (3, 3, 3, 3, 3) times, sm, K2, P12, K2, sm, [K1, P1] 5 (7, 9, 12, 14, 17) times.

Row 3: [K1, P1] 5 (7, 9, 12, 14, 17) times, sm, work Row 1 of Single Braid cable over next 16 sts, sm, K1, [P1, K1] 2 (3, 3, 3, 3, 3) times, work Row 11 for Right Side Back cable over next 22 sts.

Row 4: Work Row 12 of Right Side Back cable over next 22 sts, sm, K1, [P1, K1] 2 (3, 3, 3, 3, 3) times, sm, work Row 2 of Single Braid cable over next 16 sts, sm, [P1, K1] 5 (7, 9, 12, 14, 17) times.

The last 2 rows set seed st, Single Braid cable, Right Side Back cable, and buttonhole placket.

Keeping pattern correct, work appropriate rows on both charts until all 24 rows of Left Side Back cable are completed, ending with RS facing for next row.

Joining Row (button placket): [K1, P1] 5 (7, 9, 12, 14, 17) times, sm, work Row 7 of Single Braid cable over next 16 sts, sm, K1, [P1, K1] 2 (3, 3, 3, 3, 3) times, sm, P6, K12, [slip next 4 sts onto a cable needle and place on top of the first 4 sts of Left Side Back on st holder, with RS facing, knit through the two layers of the sts by inserting the right-hand needle into the next st on the cable needle and into the next st on the holder and knitting them together forming a pleat, rep across the 4 sts], then work rem sts from st holder as folls; K12, P6, sm, K1, [P1, K1] 2 (3, 3, 3, 3, 3) times, sm, work Row 7 of Single Braid cable over next 16 sts, sm, [P1, K1] 5 (7, 9, 12, 14, 17) times—102 (114, 122, 134, 142, 154) sts.

Next row: [K1, P1] 5 (7, 9, 12, 14, 17) times, sm, work Row 8 of Single Braid cable over next 16 sts, sm, K1, [P1, K1] 2 (3, 3, 3, 3, 3) times, sm, K6, P12, K4, P12, K6, sm, K1, [P1, K1] 2 (3, 3, 3, 3, 3) times, sm, work Row 8 of Single Braid cable over next 16 sts, sm, [K1, P1] 5 (7, 9, 12, 14, 17) times.

Next row (Center Braid cable placement): [K1, P1] 5 (7, 9, 12, 14, 17) times, sm, work Row 1 of Single Braid cable over next 16 sts, sm, K1, [P1, K1] 2 (3, 3, 3, 3, 3) times, sm, work Row 59 of Center Braid chart over next 40 sts, sm, K1, [P1, K1] 2 (3, 3, 3, 3, 3) times, sm, work Row 1 of Single Braid cable over next 16 sts, sm, [P1, K1] 5 (7, 9, 12, 14, 17) times.

Next row: [K1, P1] 5 (7, 9, 12, 14, 17) times, sm, work Row 2 of Single Braid cable over next 16 sts, sm, K1, [P1, K1] 2 (3, 3, 3, 3, 3) times, sm, work Row 60 of Center Braid chart over next 40 sts, sm, K1, [P1, K1] 2 (3, 3, 3, 3, 3) times, sm, work Row 2 of Single Braid cable over next 16 sts, sm, [P1, K1] 5 (7, 9, 12, 14, 17) times.

Then work as for front from *** to ****—110 (116, 120, 126, 134, 138) sts.

Work even in patt until armhole measures 8 (8½, 9, 9½, 10, 10½)in/20.5 (21.5, 23, 24, 25.5, 26.5)cm, ending with RS facing for next row.

Shape shoulders and back neck

Keeping patt correct, working appropriate rows on Single Braid cable chart.

Bind off 8 (9, 9, 9, 10, 10) sts, work in patt until there are 27 (29, 31, 34, 37, 39) sts on right-hand needle, place rem sts on a holder. Turn.

Work each side of neck separately.

Bind off 2 (2, 4, 7, 7, 7) sts, work in patt to end—25 (27, 27, 27, 30, 32) sts.

Bind off 8 (9, 9, 9, 10, 10) sts at beg of next row and foll RS row, then 9 (9, 9, 9, 10, 12) sts at the beg of the foll RS row.

Leave center 40 sts on back front neck holder. With RS facing, place rem sts on needle, rejoin yarn and work in patt to end—35 (38, 40, 43, 47, 49) sts.

Complete to match first side, reversing shapings.

SLEEVES
RIGHT SLEEVE

First half

Using smaller needles cast on 23 (23, 25, 25, 25, 25) sts.

Knit 2 rows.

Change to larger needles.

Row 1 (RS): K5, *P1, K1, rep from * to end.

Row 2: *K1, P1, rep from * to last 5 sts, K5.

The last 2 rows set seed st and button border.

Rep the last 2 rows 10 times more. Break off yarn and place these sts on a st holder.

Second half

Using smaller needles cast on 22 (24, 24, 24, 26, 26) sts.

Knit 2 rows.

Change to larger needles.

Row 1 (RS): *K1, P1, rep from * to last 4 sts, K4.

Row 2: K4, *P1, K1, rep from * to end.

Row 3 (buttonhole row): *K1, P1, rep from * to last 4 sts, K1, yo, K2tog, K1.

Row 4: As row 2.

Rows 5–8: As rows 1 and 2, twice.

The last 8 rows set seed st and buttonholes.

Rep the last 8 rows once, then rows 1–6 once.

Joining Row (button placket): *K1, P1, rep from * to last 4 sts, [slip the last 4 sts onto a cable needle and place on top of the first 4 sts on st holder, [with RS facing knit through the two layers of sts by inserting the right-hand needle into the next st on the cable needle and into the next st on the holder and knitting them together forming a pleat, rep across the 4 sts], then work rem sts from st holder as follows, K1, *P1, K1, rep from * to end—41 (43, 45, 45, 47, 47) sts.

**Next row: K1, *P1, K1, rep from * to end.

Rep the last row forms seed st.

Keeping seed st correct, inc 1 st at each end of next row, then every 18th (16th, 14th, 10th, 8th, 6th) row 6 (5, 6, 7, 6, 6) times, then every 0 (16th, 14th, 10th, 8th, 6th) row 0 (2, 2, 4, 6, 9) times, working inc sts into patt—55 (59, 63, 69, 73, 79) sts.

Work even in seed st pattern as set until sleeve measures 18in/45.5cm), ending with RS facing for next row.

Shape top

Keeping seed st correct, bind off 3 (3, 4, 4, 5, 5) sts at the beg of the next 2 rows—49 (53, 55, 61, 63, 69) sts.

Dec 1 st at each end of next row, then every other row 4 (10, 8, 14, 11, 17) times, then every 4th row 8 (4, 6, 2, 6, 2) times—23 (23, 25, 27, 27, 29) sts.

Work 1 row even in pattern.

Bind off 3 sts at the beg of the next 4 rows—11 (11, 13, 15, 15, 17) sts.

Bind off rem 11 (11, 13, 15, 15, 17) sts in patt. **

LEFT SLEEVE

First half

Using smaller needles, cast on 22 (24, 24, 24, 26, 26) sts.

Knit 2 rows.

Change to larger needles.

Row 1 (RS): K4, *P1, K1, rep from * to end.

Row 2: *K1, P1, rep from * to last 4 sts, K4.

Row 3 (buttonhole row): *K1, K2tog, yo, K1, *P1, K1, rep from * to end.

Row 4: Rep Row 2.

Rows 5–8: Rep Rows 1 and 2 twice.

The last 8 rows set seed st and buttonholes.

Rep the last 8 rows once, then Rows 1–6 once. Break off yarn and place these sts on a st holder.

Second half

Using smaller needles, cast on 23 (23, 25, 25, 25, 25) sts.

Knit 2 rows.

Change to larger needles.

Row 1 (RS): *K1, P1, rep from * to last 5 sts, K5.

Row 2: K5, *P1, K1, rep from * to end.

The last 2 rows set seed st and button border.

Rep the last 2 rows 10 times more.

Joining Row (button placket): K1, *P1, K1, rep from * to last 4 sts, [slip the last 4 sts onto a cable needle and place behind the first 4 sts on st holder, with RS facing knit through the two layers of sts by inserting the right-hand needle into the next st on the left-hand needle and into the next st on the holder and knit them together forming a pleat, rep across the 4 sts], then work rem sts from st holder as follows, *P1, K1, rep from * to end—41 (43, 45, 45, 47, 47) sts.

Now work as given for Right Sleeve from ** to **.

FINISHING

Join shoulder seams.

Neckband

With RS facing and using a set of DPNs, pick up and knit 20 sts down left side of front neck, work across the 36 sts from front st holder as follows: [K1, K2tog, K1] 9 times, 20 sts up right side of front neck, and 8 sts down right side of back neck, work across the 40 sts from back st holder as follows: [K1, K2tog, K1] 10 times, then pick up and knit 8 sts up left side of back neck—113 sts.

Join into round, taking care not to twist the sts; pm at beg of first round.

Rnd 1: P.

Rnd 2: K.

Bind off as if to purl.

Sew in sleeves, being careful to sew right sleeve to right armhole and left sleeve to left armhole. Join sleeve and side seams. Sew on buttons to correspond with all buttonholes.

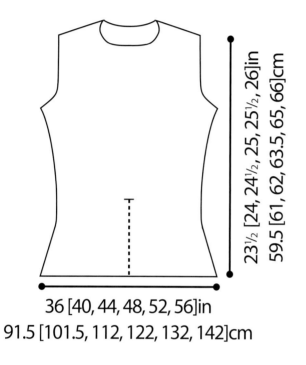

23½ [24, 24½, 25, 25½, 26]in
59.5 [61, 62, 63.5, 65, 66]cm

36 [40, 44, 48, 52, 56]in
91.5 [101.5, 112, 122, 132, 142]cm

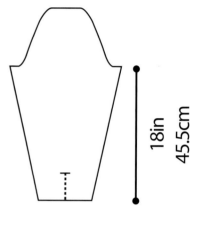

18in
45.5cm

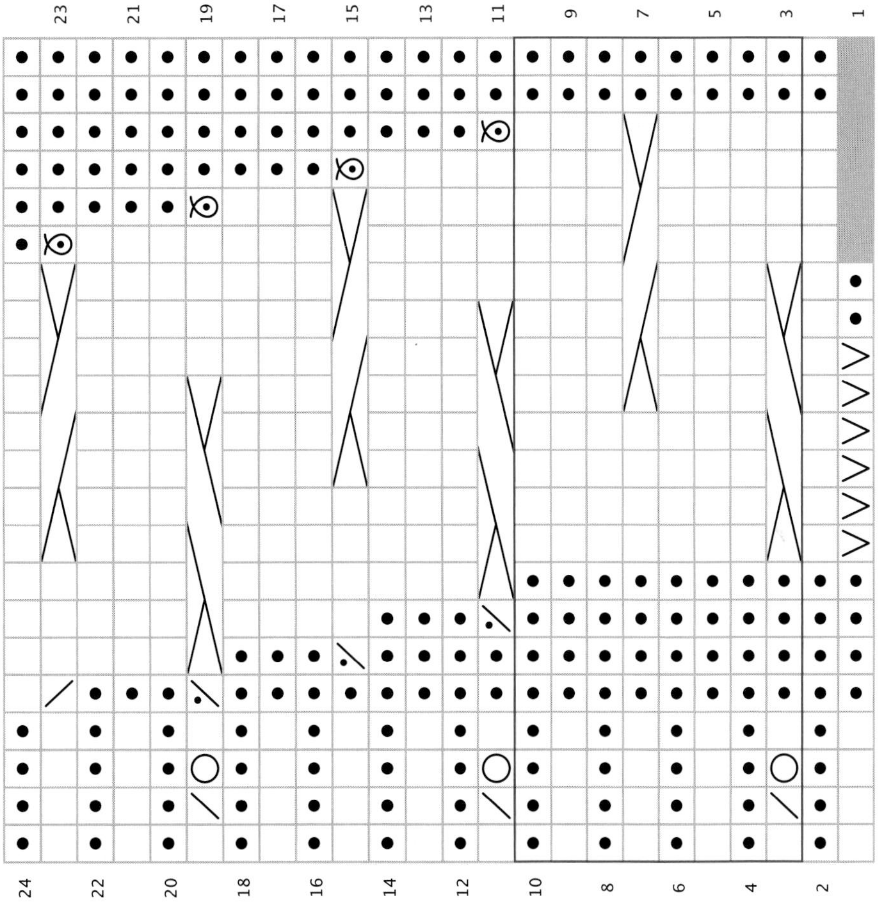

LEFT SIDE BACK CABLE CHART

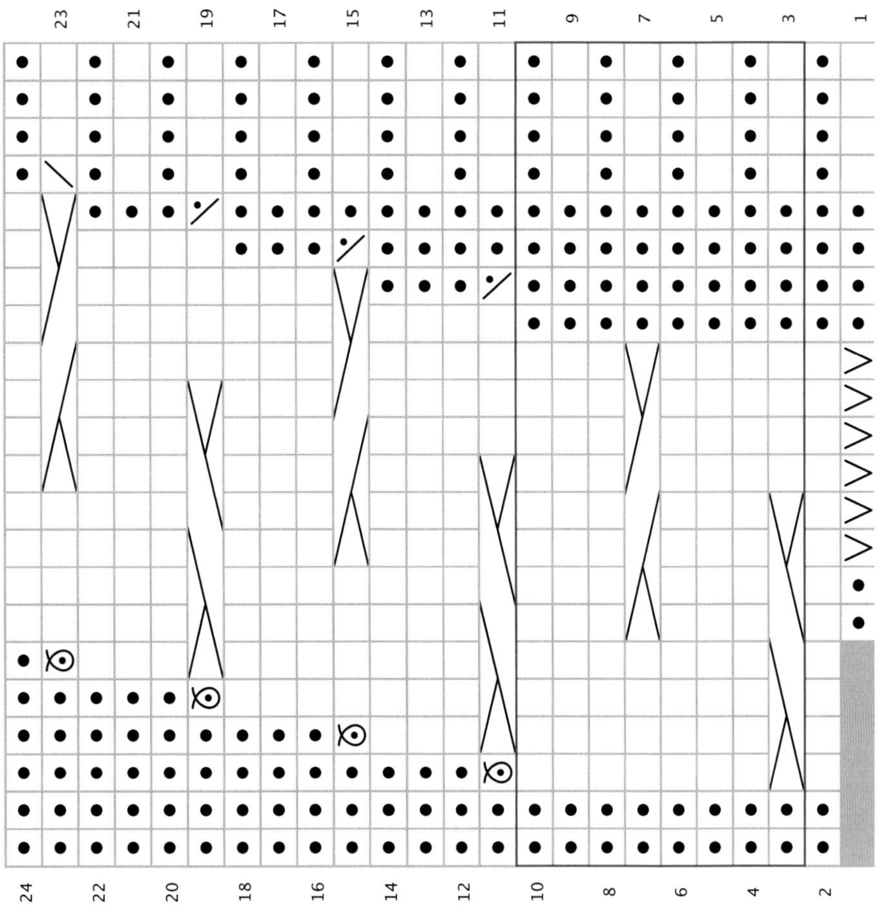

RIGHT SIDE BACK CABLE CHART

KEY

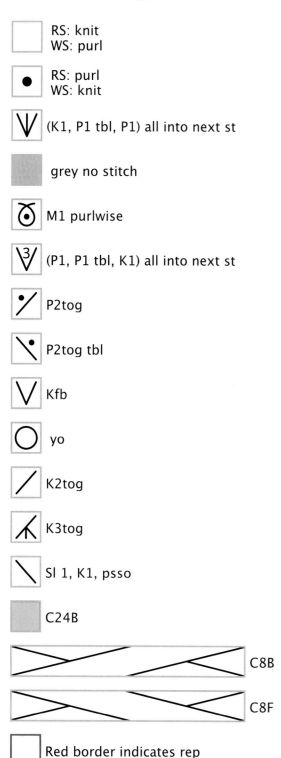

RS: knit
WS: purl

RS: purl
WS: knit

(K1, P1 tbl, P1) all into next st

grey no stitch

M1 purlwise

(P1, P1 tbl, K1) all into next st

P2tog

P2tog tbl

Kfb

yo

K2tog

K3tog

Sl 1, K1, psso

C24B

C8B

C8F

Red border indicates rep

CENTER BRAID CABLE CHART

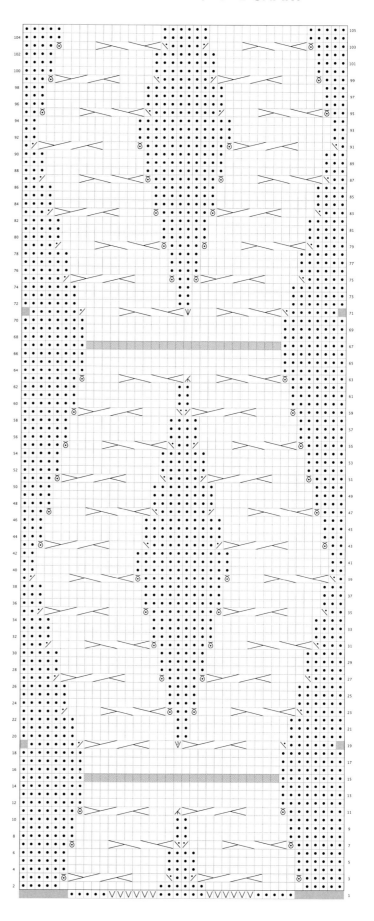

HIP BRAID CABLE CHART

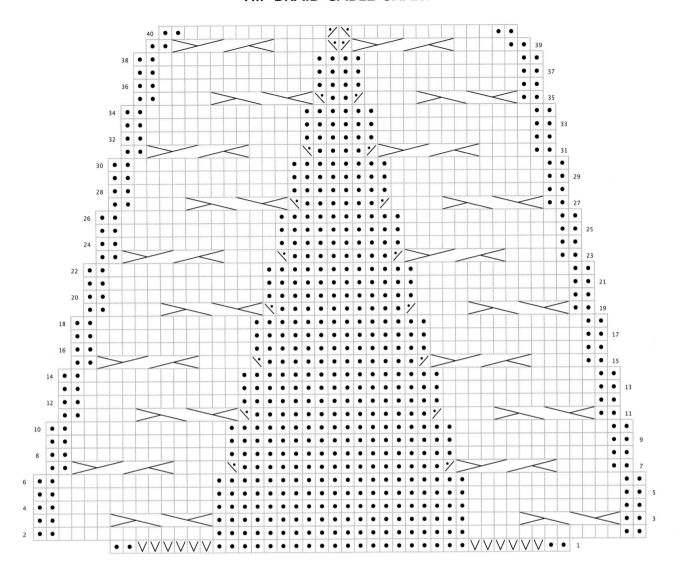

SINGLE BRAID CABLE CHART

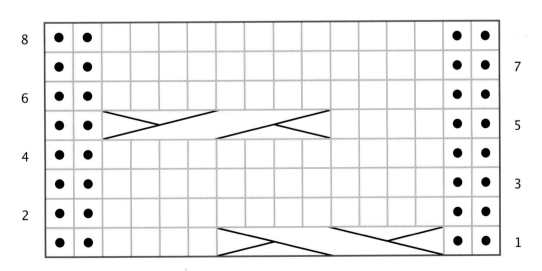

OVERSIZED WRAP

Skill Level ★★

MEASUREMENTS AND YARN

Size	One size only	
Width (approximately)	25 63.5	in cm
Full Length (approximately)	63 160	in cm
Cascade Yarns® Baby Alpaca Chunky (100% alpaca) in #596 Brown	15	3½oz/100g 108yds/99m hanks

OTHER MATERIALS

• 1 pair US 10 (6mm) knitting needles OR SIZE TO OBTAIN GAUGE

• Cable needle

• Shawl pin to fasten

Gauge 14 sts and 18 rows = 4in/10cm in St st using US 10 (6mm) needles.

TAKE TIME TO CHECK GAUGE.

SPECIAL ABBREVIATIONS

C6B: Slip next 3 sts onto a cable needle and hold at back, K3, then K3 from cable needle.

C4BP: Slip next st onto a cable needle and hold at back, K3, then P1 from cable needle.

C4FP: Slip next 3 sts onto a cable needle and hold at front, P1, then K3 from cable needle.

C4BK: Slip next st onto cable needle and hold at back, K3, then K1 from cable needle.

C4FK: Slip next 3 sts onto a cable needle and hold at front, K1, then K3 from cable needle.

WRAP

Cast on 138 sts.

BOTTOM WELT

Row 1 (RS): [K1, P1] 7 times, K2, P2, K2, *P1, [K1, P1] 3 times, K2, P2, K2 rep from * 7 times more, [P1, K1] 7 times.

Row 2: [K1, P1] 3 times, K2, [P1, K1] 3 times, P2, K2, P2, *[K1, P1] 3 times, K1, P2, K2, P2, rep from * 7 times more, [K1, P1] 3 times, K2, [P1, K1] 3 times.

Rep last 2 rows 10 times more.

CABLE PATTERN

Beginning and ending rows as indicated, work Rows 1 and 2 from chart, then rep Rows 3–46 nine times more.

TOP WELT

Row 1 (RS): [K1, P1] 7 times, K2, P2, K2, *P1, [K1, P1] 3 times, K2, P2, K2, rep from * 7 times more, [P1, K1] 7 times.

Row 2: [K1, P1] 3 times, K2, [P1, K1] 3 times, P2, K2, P2, *[K1, P1] 3 times, K1, P2, K2, P2, rep from * 7 times more, [K1, P1] 3 times, K2, [P1, K1] 3 times.

Rep last 2 rows 10 times more.

Bind off in patt.

FINISHING

Weave in ends of yarn.

OVERSIZED WRAP CHART

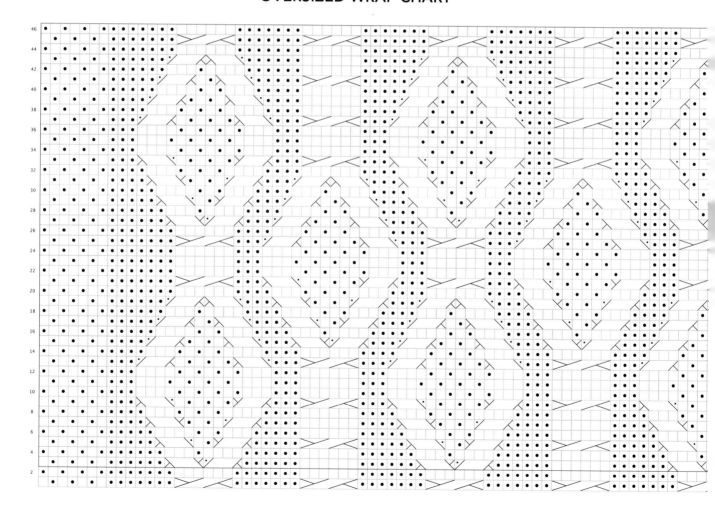

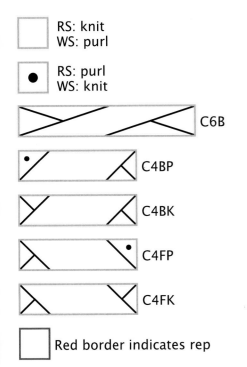

	RS: knit WS: purl
	RS: purl WS: knit
	C6B
	C4BP
	C4BK
	C4FP
	C4FK
	Red border indicates rep

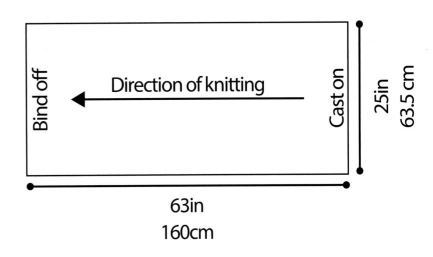

Bind off — Direction of knitting — Cast on

25in
63.5 cm

63in
160cm

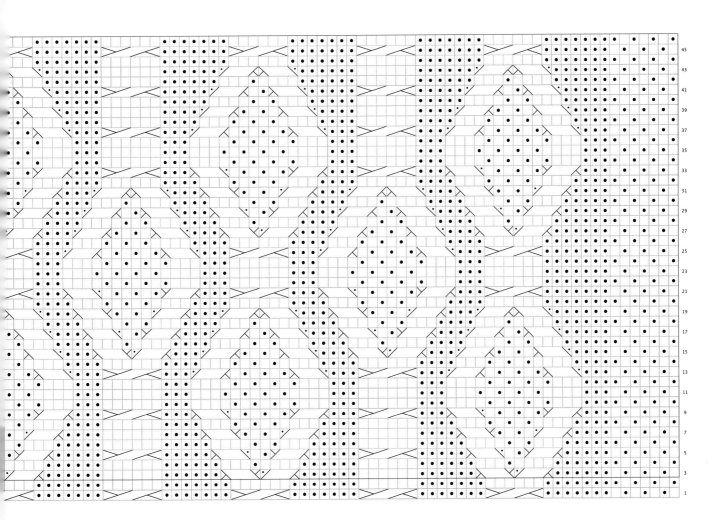

TOTE
FRONT

Cast on 34 sts for lower edge.

Row 1 [WS]: P8, K2, [P6, K2] twice, P8.

Row 2: K1, m1, K7, P2, [K6, P2] twice, K7, m1, K1—36 sts.

Row 3: P1, m1, P8, K2, [P6, K2] twice, P8, m1, P1—38 sts.

Row 4: K1, m1, K9, P2, C6B, P2, C6F, P2, K9, m1, K1—40 sts.

Row 5: P1, m1, P10, K2, [P6, K2] twice, P10, m1, P1—42 sts.

Row 6: K1, m1, K11, P2, [K6, P2] twice, K11, m1, K1—44 sts.

Row 7: P1, m1, P12, K2, [P6, K2] twice, P12, m1, P1—46 sts.

Row 8: K1, m1, K13, P2, [K6, P2] twice, K13, m1, K1—48 sts.

Row 9: P1, m1, P14, K2, [P6, K2] twice, P14, m1, P1—50 sts.

Row 10: K1, m1, K15, P2, [K6, P2] twice, K15, m1, K1—52 sts.

Row 11: P1, m1, P16, K2, [P6, K2] twice, P16, m1, P1—54 sts.

Row 12: K18, P2, C6B, P2, C6F, P2, K18.

Row 13: P18, K2, [P6, K2] twice, P18.

Row 14: K18, P2, [K6, P2] twice, K18.

Rows 15–19: Rep Rows 13 and 14 twice more, then Row 13 once more.

Row 20: K1, skpo, K15, P2, C6B, P2, C6F, P2, K15, K2tog, K1—52 sts.

Row 21: P17, K2, [P6, K2] twice, P17.

Row 22: K17, P2, [K6, P2] twice, K17.

Row 23: Rep Row 21.

Row 24: K1, skpo, K14, P2, [K6, P2] twice, K14, K2tog, K1—50 sts.

Row 25: P16, K2, [P6, K2] twice, P16.

Row 26: K16, P2, [K6, P2] twice, K16.

Row 27: Rep Row 25.

Row 28: K1, skpo, K13, P2, C6B, P2, C6F, P2, K13, K2tog, K1—48 sts.

Row 29: P15, K2, [P6, K2] twice, P15.

Row 30: K15, P2, [K6, P2] twice, K15.

Row 31: Rep Row 29.

Row 32: K1, skpo, K12, P2, [K6, P2] twice, K12, K2tog, K1—46 sts.

Row 33: P14, K2, [P6, K2] twice, P14.

Row 34: K14, P2, [K6, P2] twice, K14.

Row 35: Rep Row 33.

Row 36: K1, skpo, K11, P2, C6B, P2, C6F, P2, K11, K2tog, K1—44 sts.

Row 37: P13, K2, [P6, K2] twice, P13.

Row 38: K13, P2, [K6, P2] twice, K13.

Row 39: Rep Row 37.

Row 40: K1, skpo, K10, P2, [K6, P2] twice, K10, K2tog, K1—42 sts.

Row 41: P12, K2, [P6, K2] twice, P12.

Row 42: K12, P2, [K6, P2] twice, K12.

Row 43: Rep Row 41.

Row 44: K1, skpo, K9, P2, C6B, P2, C6F, P2, K9, K2tog, K1—40 sts.

Row 45: P11, K2, [P6, K2] twice, P11.

Row 46: K11, P2, [K6, P2] twice, K11.

Row 47: Rep Row 45.

Row 48: K1, skpo, K8, P2, [K6, P2] twice, K8, K2tog, K1—38 sts.

Row 49: P10, K2, [P6, K2] twice, P10.

Row 50: K10, P2, [K6, P2] twice, K10.

Row 51: Rep Row 49.

Row 52: K1, skpo, K7, P2, C6B, P2, C6F, P2, K7, K2tog, K1—36 sts.

Row 53: P9, K2, [P6, K2] twice, P9.

Row 54: K9, P2, [K6, P2] twice, K9.

Row 55: Rep Row 53.

Row 56: K1, skpo, K9, [K2tog] twice, K4, [K2tog] twice, K9, K2tog, K1—30 sts.

Work 2 rows in Gst. **

Bind off as if to knit.

BACK

Work as given for front to **.

Work buttonhole flap: Bind off 13 sts, K3, bind off rem 13 sts—4 sts.

Working on these 4 sts only, rejoin yarn and work 10 rows in Gst.

Next row: K2tog, [yo] twice, skpo.

Next row: Knit, working into front of first yo, then into the back of the second yo.

Work 1 more row in Gst.

Bind off as if to knit.

HANDLES (Make 2)

Using yarn held doubled, cast on 43 sts and work 5 rows in Gst.

Bind off as if to knit.

FINISHING

Join front to back along sides and lower edge, leaving bound-off edges open. Pin row ends of each handle to inside of bag. Cut two pieces of lining material ½in/1.25cm larger all around than the knitting. Join the lining pieces right sides together by machine or hand, using a ½in/1.25cm seam allowance. Fold ½in/1.25cm at top of lining to wrong side. Place lining in bag with wrong side of lining against wrong side of bag, and slipstitch in place just below the bound-off edge. Sew on button.

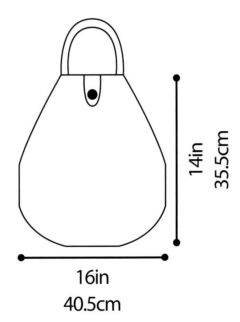

14in
35.5cm

16in
40.5cm

SWEATER DRESS

Skill Level ★★

MEASUREMENTS AND YARN

To fit bust	32–34 81.5–86.5	36–38 91.5–96.5	40–42 101.5–106.5	44–46 112–117	48–50 122–127	52–54 132–137	in cm
Actual size	37½ 95.5	40 101.5	43½ 110.5	47½ 120.5	51 129.5	57 145	in cm
Full Length (approximately)	32 81.5	34 86.5	34 86.5	34½ 87.5	36½ 92.5	37 94	in cm
Sleeve Length (adjustable)	18 45.5	18 45.5	18 45.5	18 45.5	18 45.5	18 45.5	in cm
Juniper Moon Farm Moonshine (40% wool, 40% alpaca, 20% silk) in #13 June Bug	8	9	10	11	12	13	3½oz/100g 197yds/180m balls

OTHER MATERIALS

- 1 pair US 6 (4mm) knitting needles OR SIZE TO OBTAIN GAUGE
- 1 pair US 7 (4.5mm) knitting needles OR SIZE TO OBTAIN GAUGE
- 1 US 6 (4mm) 32in/81.5cm circular needle OR SIZE TO OBTAIN GAUGE
- Cable needle
- Stitch holders

Gauge: 26 sts and 28 rows = 4in/10cm in patt using US 7 (4.5mm) needles.

TAKE TIME TO CHECK GAUGE.

SPECIAL ABBREVIATIONS

C4B: slip next 2 sts onto a cable needle and hold at back, K2, then K2 from cable needle.
C4F: slip next 2 sts onto a cable needle and hold at front, K2, then K2 from cable needle.

DRESS

FRONT

Using smaller needles, cast on 128 (139, 150, 161, 172, 194) sts.

Row 1 (RS): K1, *P2, K1 tbl, [P2, K2] twice, rep from * to last 6 sts, P2, K1 tbl, P2, K1.

Row 2: P1, *K2, P1 tbl, [K2, P2] twice, rep from * to last 6 sts, K2, P1 tbl, K2, P1.

These 2 rows form ribbing.

Work 20 more rows in ribbing, ending with RS facing for next row.

Change to larger needles.

Rows 1 and 5 (RS): K1, *P2, K1 tbl, P2, K6, rep from * to last 6 sts, P2, K1 tbl, P2, K1.

Rows 2, 4, 6 and 8: P1, *K2, P1 tbl, K2, P6, rep from * to last 6 sts, K2, P1 tbl, K2, P1.

Row 3: K1, *P2, K1 tbl, P2, K2, C4B, rep from * to last 6 sts, P2, K1 tbl, P2, K1.

Row 7: K1, *P2, K1 tbl, P2, C4F, K2, rep from * to last 6 sts, P2, K1 tbl, P2, K1.

These 8 rows form cable patt.

Work even in patt as set until front measures 9 (9, 10, 10, 11, 11)in/23 (23, 25.5, 25.5, 28, 28)cm, ending with Row 8 of cable patt, with RS facing for next row.

Waist shaping

The waist decreases are incorporated inside the cable pattern throughout the next section. Stitches will be decreased in the Rev St st columns between the cables on the next and every following 4th row.

Row 1 (RS): K1, P2tog, K1 tbl, P2, K6, [P2, K1 tbl, P2, K6] 10 (11, 12, 13, 14, 16) times, P2, K1 tbl, P2tog tbl, K1—126 (137, 148, 159, 170, 192) sts.

Working 1 st in Rev St st (instead of 2 sts) where dec was worked, work 3 rows in patt.

Row 5: K1, P1, K1 tbl, P2tog, K6, [P2, K1 tbl, P2, K6] 10 (11, 12, 13, 14, 16) times, P2tog tbl, K1 tbl, P1, K1—124 (135, 146, 157, 168, 190) sts.

Working 1 st in Rev St st (instead of 2 sts) where dec was worked, work 3 rows in patt.

Row 9: K1, P1, K1 tbl, P1, K6, P2tog, K1 tbl, P2, K6, [P2, K1 tbl, P2, K6] 8 (9, 10, 11, 12, 14) times, P2, K1 tbl, P2tog tbl, K6, P1, K1 tbl, P1, K1—122 (133, 144, 155, 166, 188) sts.

Working 1 st in Rev St st (instead of 2 sts) where dec was worked, work 3 rows in patt.

Row 13: K1, P1, K1 tbl, P1, K6, P1, K1 tbl, P2tog, K6, [P2, K1 tbl, P2, K6] 8 (9, 10, 11, 12, 14) times, P2tog tbl, K1 tbl, P1, K6, P1, K1 tbl, P1, K1—120 (131, 142, 153, 164, 186) sts.

Working 1 st in Rev St st (instead of 2 sts) where dec was worked, work 3 rows in patt.

Row 17: K1, [P1, K1 tbl, P1, K6] twice, P2tog, K1 tbl, P2, K6, [P2, K1 tbl, P2, K6] 6 (7, 8: 9, 10, 12) times, P2, K1 tbl, P2tog tbl, [K6, P1, K1 tbl, P1] twice, K1—118 (129, 140, 151, 162, 184) sts.

Working 1 st in Rev St st (instead of 2 sts) where dec was worked, work 3 rows in patt.

Row 21: K1, [P1, K1 tbl, P1, K6] twice, P1, K1 tbl, P2tog, K6, [P2, K1 tbl, P2, K6] 6 (7, 8, 9, 10, 12) times, P2tog tbl, K1 tbl, P1, [K6, P1, K1 tbl, P1] twice, K1—116 (127, 138, 149, 160, 182) sts.

Working 1 st in Rev St st (instead of 2 sts) where dec was worked, work 3 rows in patt.

Row 25: K1, [P1, K1 tbl, P1, K6] 3 times, P2tog, K1 tbl, P2, K6, [P2, K1 tbl, P2, K6] 4 (5, 6, 7, 8, 10) times, P2, K1 tbl, P2tog tbl, [K6, P1, K1 tbl, P1] 3 times, K1—114 (125, 136, 147, 158, 180) sts.

Working 1 st in Rev St st (instead of 2 sts) where dec was worked, work 3 rows in patt.

Row 29: K1, [P1, K1 tbl, P1, K6] 3 times, P1, K1 tbl, P2tog, K6, [P2, K1 tbl, P2, K6] 4 (5, 6, 7, 8, 10) times, P2tog tbl, K1 tbl, P1, [K6, P1, K1 tbl, P1] 3 times, K1—112 (123, 134, 145, 156, 178) sts.

Working 1 st in Rev St st (instead of 2 sts) where dec was worked, work 3 rows in patt.

Row 33: K1, [P1, K1 tbl, P1, K6] 4 times, P2tog, K1 tbl, P2, K6, [P2, K1 tbl, P2, K6] 2 (3, 4, 5, 6, 8) times, P2, K1 tbl, P2tog tbl, (K6, P1, K1 tbl, P1) 4 times, K1—110 [121, 132, 143, 154, 176] sts.

Working 1 st in Rev St st (instead of 2 sts) where dec was worked, work 3 rows in patt.

Row 37: K1, [P1, K1 tbl, P1, K6] 4 times, P1, K1 tbl, P2tog, K6, [P2, K1 tbl, P2, K6] 2 (3, 4, 5, 6, 8) times, P2tog tbl, K1 tbl, P1, [K6, P1, K1 tbl, P1] 4 times, K1—108 (119, 130, 141, 152, 174) sts.

Working 1 st in Rev St st (instead of 2 sts) where dec was worked, work 3 rows in patt.

1st size only

Row 41: K1, [P1, K1 tbl, P1, K6] 5 times, P2tog, K1 tbl, P2, K6, P2, K1 tbl, P2tog tbl, [K6, P1, K1 tbl, P1] 5 times, K1—106 sts.

Working 1 st in Rev St st (instead of 2 sts) where dec was worked, work 3 rows in patt.

Row 45: K1, [P1, K1 tbl, P1, K6] 5 times, P1, K1 tbl, P2tog, K6, P2tog tbl, K1 tbl, P1, [K6, P1, K1 tbl, P1] 5 times, K1—104 sts.

2nd, 3rd, 4th, 5th & 6th sizes only

Row 41: K1, [P1, K1 tbl, P1, K6] 5 times, P2tog, K1 tbl, P2, K6, [P2, K1 tbl, P2, K6] (1, 2, 3, 4, 6) times, P2, K1 tbl, P2tog tbl, [K6, P1, K1 tbl, P1] 5 times, K1—(117, 128, 139, 150, 172) sts.

Working 1 st in Rev St st (instead of 2 sts) where dec was worked, work 3 rows in patt.

Row 45: K1, [P1, K1 tbl, P1, K6] 5 times, P1, K1 tbl, P2tog, K6, [P2, K1 tbl, P2, K6] (1, 2, 3, 4, 6) times, P2tog tbl, K1 tbl, P1, [K6, P1, K1 tbl, P1] 5 times, K1—(115, 126, 137, 148, 170) sts.

All sizes

Working 1 st in Rev St st (instead of 2 sts) where dec was worked, work even in patt until work measures 18 (19, 19, 19, 20, 20)in/45.5 (48, 48, 48, 50.5, 50.5)cm, ending with Row 8 of cable patt, with RS facing for next row.

Bust shaping

Bust increases are incorporated inside the cable pattern throughout the next section. Stitches will be increased in the Rev St st columns between the cables on the next and every following 4th row.

1st size only

Row 1 (RS): K1, [P1, K1 tbl, P1, K6] 5 times, P1, K1 tbl, Pfb, K6, Pfb, K1 tbl, P1, [K6, P1, K1 tbl, P1] 5 times, K1—106 sts.

Working 2 sts in Rev St st (instead of 1 st) where inc was worked, 3 rows in patt.

Row 5: K1, [P1, K1 tbl, P1, K6] 5 times, Pfb, K1 tbl, P2, K6, P2, K1 tbl, Pfb, [K6, P1, K1 tbl, P1] 5 times, K1—108 sts.

2nd, 3rd, 4th, 5th & 6th sizes only

Row 1 (RS): K1, [P1, K1 tbl, P1, K6] 5 times, P1, K1 tbl, Pfb, K6, [P2, K1 tbl, P2, K6] (1, 2, 3, 4, 6) times, Pfb, K1 tbl, P1, [K6, P1, K1 tbl, P1] 5 times, K1—(117, 128, 139, 150, 172) sts.

Working 2 sts in Rev St st (instead of 1 st) where inc was worked, 3 rows in patt.

Row 5: K1, [P1, K1 tbl, P1, K6] 5 times, Pfb, K1 tbl, P2, K6, [P2, K1 tbl, P2, K6] (1, 2, 3, 4, 6) times, P2, K1 tbl, Pfb, (K6, P1, K1 tbl, P1) 5 times, K1—(119, 130, 141, 152, 174) sts.

All sizes

Working 2 sts in Rev St st (instead of 1 st) where inc was worked, 3 rows in patt.

Row 9: K1, [P1, K1 tbl, P1, K6] 4 times, P1, K1 tbl, Pfb, K6, [P2, K1 tbl, P2, K6] 2 (3, 4, 5, 6, 8) times, Pfb, K1 tbl, P1, [K6, P1, K1 tbl, P1] 4 times, K1—110 (121, 132, 143, 154, 176) sts.

Working 2 sts in Rev St st (instead of 1 st) where inc was worked, 3 rows in patt.

Row 13: K1, [P1, K1 tbl, P1, K6] 4 times, Pfb, K1 tbl, P2, K6, [P2, K1 tbl, P2, K6] 2 (3, 4, 5, 6, 8) times, P2, K1 tbl,

Pfb, [K6, P1, K1 tbl, P1] 4 times, K1—112 (123, 134, 145, 156, 178) sts.

Working 2 sts in Rev St st (instead of 1 st) where inc was worked, 3 rows in patt.

Row 17: K1, [P1, K1 tbl, P1, K6] 3 times, P1, K1 tbl, Pfb, K6, [P2, K1 tbl, P2, K6] 4 (5, 6, 7, 8, 10) times, Pfb, K1 tbl, P1, [K6, P1, K1 tbl, P1] 3 times, K1—114 (125, 136, 147, 158, 180) sts.

Working 2 sts in Rev St st (instead of 1 st) where inc was worked, 3 rows in patt.

Row 21: K1, [P1, K1 tbl, P1, K6] 3 times, Pfb, K1 tbl, P2, K6, [P2, K1 tbl, P2, K6] 4 (5, 6, 7, 8, 10) times, P2, K1 tbl, Pfb, [K6, P1, K1 tbl, P1] 3 times, K1—116 (127, 138, 149, 160, 182) sts.

Working 2 sts in Rev St st (instead of 1 st) where inc was worked, 3 rows in patt.

Row 25: K1, [P1, K1 tbl, P1, K6] twice, P1, K1 tbl, Pfb, K6, [P2, K1 tbl, P2, K6] 6 (7, 8, 9, 10, 12) times, Pfb, K1 tbl, P1, [K6, P1, K1 tbl, P1] twice, K1—118 (129, 140, 151, 162, 184) sts.

Working 2 sts in Rev St st (instead of 1 st) where inc was worked, 3 rows in patt.

Row 29: K1, [P1, K1 tbl, P1, K6] twice, Pfb, K1 tbl, P2, K6, [P2, K1 tbl, P2, K6] 6 (7, 8, 9, 10, 12) times, P2, K1 tbl, Pfb, [K6, P1, K1 tbl, P1] twice, K1—120 (131, 142, 153, 164, 186) sts.

Working 2 sts in Rev St st (instead of 1 st) where inc was worked, 3 rows in patt.

Row 33: K1, P1, K1 tbl, P1, K6, P1, K1 tbl, Pfb, K6, [P2, K1 tbl, P2, K6] 8 (9, 10, 11, 12, 14) times, Pfb, K1 tbl, P1, K6, P1, K1 tbl, P1, K1—122 (133, 144, 155, 166, 188) sts.

Row 34: Work in cable patt as set—122 (133, 144, 155, 166, 188) sts.**

Work even in cable patt until piece measures 23 (24¼, 24¼, 24¼, 25½, 25½)in/58.5 (61.5, 61.5, 61.5, 64.5, 64.5) cm from cast on edge, ending with Row 2 of cable patt, with RS facing for next row.

Neck shaping

Work patt over 61 (66, 72, 77, 83, 94) sts, place rem sts on a holder, turn. Work each side of neck separately, keeping cable patt correct as set.

Work 1 row even.

1st, 2nd, 3rd & 4th sizes only

Dec 1 st at neck edge on next row, then every other row 9 times—51 (56, 62, 67) sts.

Work 1 row even, ending with RS facing for next row.

5th & 6th sizes only

Dec 1 st at neck edge on next row, then every row 8 times, then on every other row 5 times—69 (80) sts.

Work 1 row even, ending with RS facing for next row.

All sizes

Shape armhole

Keeping cable patt correct, bind off 5 (7, 7, 8, 10, 11) sts and dec 1 st at neck edge—45 (48, 54, 58, 58, 68) sts.

Work 1 row even.

Dec 1 st at each end of next row, then every other row 9 (9, 12, 12, 11, 17) times, ending with RS facing for next row—25 (28, 28, 32, 34, 32) sts.

2nd size only

Dec 1 st at armhole edge once. Work 1 row even—27 sts.

All sizes

Neck shaping (cont)

Keeping cable patt correct, dec 1 st at neck edge only on next row, then every other row 1 (0, 6, 9, 18, 14) times, then on every 4th row 6 (7, 4, 3, 0, 0) times—17 (19, 17, 19, 15, 17) sts.

Work even until piece measures 8 (8½, 9, 9½, 10, 10½) in/20.5 (21.5, 23, 24, 25.5, 26.5)cm from armhole bind off, ending with RS facing for next row.

Shape shoulder

Bind off 5 (7, 5, 7, 5, 5) sts at beg of next row and following RS row, then bind off 7 (5, 7, 5, 5, 7) sts at beg of next RS row.

Place sts from holder on needle. With RS facing, rejoin yarn and bind off 0 (1, 0, 1, 0, 0) sts at V neck edge, then work in cable patt to end—61 (67, 72, 78, 83, 94) sts.

Complete to match first side, reversing shapings.

BACK

Work as given for Front to **.

Work even until back measures the same as front to start of armhole shaping, ending with RS facing for next row.

Shape armholes

Keeping cable patt correct, bind off 5 (7, 7, 8, 10, 11) sts at the beg of the next 2 rows—112 (119, 130, 139, 146, 166) sts.

Dec 1 st at each end of next row, then every other row 9 (10, 12, 12, 11, 17) times, ending with RS facing for next row—92 (97, 104, 113, 122, 130) sts.

Cont even in patt until back measures 8 rows less than front to start of shoulder shaping, ending with RS facing for next row.

Back neck shaping

Work 31 (33, 34, 37, 35, 38) sts; place rem sts on a holder; turn.

Work each side of neck separately, keeping patt correct.

Bind off 4 (4, 5, 6, 7, 8) sts at beg of next row—27 (29, 29, 31, 28, 30) sts.

Work 1 row even.

Bind off 5 (5, 7, 7, 8, 8) sts at beg next row—22 (24, 22, 24, 20, 22) sts.

Dec 1 st at neck edge on next 4 rows, ending with RS facing for next row—18 (20, 18, 20, 16, 18) sts.

Shape shoulder

Keeping patt correct, bind off 5 (7, 5, 7, 5, 5) sts, work in patt to last 2 sts, work 2 sts tog for decrease—12 (12, 12, 12, 10, 12) sts.

Work 1 row even.

Bind off 5 (7, 5, 7, 5, 5) sts at beg of next row; work 1 row even.

Bind off 7 (5, 7, 5, 5, 7) sts at beg of next row.

Leave center 30 (31, 36, 39, 52, 54) sts on holder for back neck; place rem sts on needle with RS facing. Rejoin yarn, work in patt to end—31 (33, 34, 37, 35, 38) sts.

Complete to match first side, reversing shaping.

SLEEVES (Make 2)

Using smaller needles, cast on 51 (55, 57, 59, 61, 61) sts.

Row 1 (RS): K0 (0, 0, 1, 2, 2), P0 (1, 2, 2, 2, 2), K1 (2, 2, 2, 2, 2), *P2, K1 tbl, [P2, K2] twice, rep from * to last 6 (8, 9, 10, 11, 11) sts, P2, K1 tbl, P2, K1 (2, 2, 2, 2, 2), P0 (1, 2, 2, 2, 2), K0 (0, 0, 1, 2, 2).

Row 2: P0 (0, 0, 1, 2, 2), K0(1, 2, 2, 2, 2), P1 (2, 2, 2, 2, 2,) *K2, P1 tbl, [K2, P2] twice, rep from * to last 6 (8, 9, 10, 11, 11) sts, K2, P1 tbl, K2, P1 (2, 2, 2, 2, 2), K0 (1, 2, 2, 2, 2), P0 (0, 0, 1, 2, 2).

These 2 rows form the ribbing.

Work 20 more rows in ribbing, ending with RS facing for next row.

Change to larger needles.

NOTE: The sleeve increases begin on the third row of the cable patt.

Row 1 (RS): K1 (3, 4, 5, 6, 6), [P2, K1 tbl, P2, K6] 4 times, P2, K1 tbl, P2, K1 (3, 4, 5, 6, 6).

Row 2: P1 (3, 4, 5, 6, 6), [K2, P1 tbl, K2, P6] 4 times, K2, P1 tbl, K2, P1 (3, 4, 5, 6, 6).

Row 3: Inc in first st, K0 (2, 3, 4, 5, 5), [P2, K1 tbl, P2, K2, C4B] 4 times, P2, K1 tbl, P2, K0 (2, 3, 4, 5, 5), inc in last st—53 (57, 59, 61, 63, 63) sts.

Rows 4 and 6: K0 (0, 0, 0, 1, 1), P2 (4, 5, 6, 6, 6), [K2, P1 tbl, K2, P6] 4 times, K2, P1 tbl, K2, P2 (4, 5, 6, 6, 6), K0 (0, 0, 0, 1, 1).

Row 5: P0 (0, 0, 0, 1, 1), K2 (4, 5, 6, 6, 6), [P2, K1 tbl, P2, K6] 4 times, P2, K1 tbl, P2, K2 (4, 5, 6, 6, 6), P0 (0, 0, 0, 1, 1).

Row 7: Inc in first st 0 (0, 1, 1, 1, 1) time, K2 (4, 4, 5, 0, 0), [C4F, K2] 0 (0, 0, 0, 1, 1) time, [P2, K1 tbl, P2, C4F, K2] 4 times, P2, K1 tbl, P2, K2 (4, 4, 5, 0, 0), [C4F, K2] 0 (0, 0, 0, 1, 1) time, inc in last st 0 (0, 1, 1, 1, 1) time—53 (57, 61, 63, 65, 65) sts.

Row 8: K0 (0, 1, 1, 2, 2), P2 (4, 6, 6, 6, 6), [K2, P1 tbl, K2, P6] 4 times, K2, P1 tbl, K2, P2 (4, 6, 6, 6, 6), K0 (0, 1, 1, 2, 2).

These 8 rows form cable patt.

Keeping patt correct, and working increased sts into the patt, inc 1 st at each end of next (next, 3rd, 3rd, 3rd, 3rd) row, then every 8th (8th, 4th, 4th, 3rd, 3rd) row 2 (2, 5, 14, 2, 18) times, then every 6th (6th, 6th, 6th, 4th, 4th) row 9 (9, 8, 2, 16, 4) times—77 (81, 89, 97, 103, 111) sts.

Work even in patt until sleeve measures 18in/45.5cm, ending with RS facing for next row.

Shape top

Keeping patt correct, bind off 5 (7, 7, 8, 10, 11) sts at the beg of the next 2 rows—67 (67, 75, 81, 83, 89) sts.

Dec 1 st at each end of next 3 (3, 7, 11, 9, 13) rows, then every other row 14 (14, 13, 11, 14, 12) times—33 (33, 35, 37, 37, 39) sts.

Work 1 row even.

Bind off 3 sts at the beg of the next 4 rows—21 (21, 23, 25, 25, 27) sts.

Bind off rem 21 (21, 23, 25, 25, 27) sts in patt.

NECKBAND

Join both shoulder seams.

Using circular needle, with RS facing and starting from the bottom of the V neck, pick up and K74 (77, 90, 94, 102, 106) sts along right front neck, 16 (17, 21, 24, 27, 28) sts down right side of back neck, K30 (31, 36, 39, 52, 54) sts from back neck stitch holder, then 16 (17, 21, 24, 27, 28) sts up left side of back neck, then 74 (76, 90, 93, 102, 106) sts down left edge of V neck. Do not join—210 (218, 258, 274, 310, 322) sts.

Row 1 (RS): K1, *K2, P2, rep from * to last st, K1.

Rep Row 1 until neckband measures 3in/7.5cm.

Bind off loosely in patt.

FINISHING

Overlap edges of the neckband and seam in place, using picture as a guide.

Sew sleeves into armholes. Join side and sleeve seams.

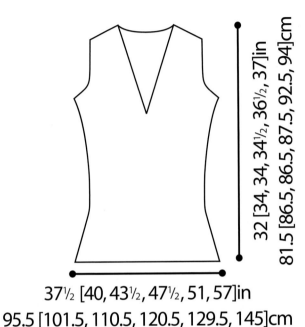

32 [34, 34, 34½, 36½, 37]in
81.5 [86.5, 86.5, 87.5, 92.5, 94]cm

37½ [40, 43½, 47½, 51, 57]in
95.5 [101.5, 110.5, 120.5, 129.5, 145]cm

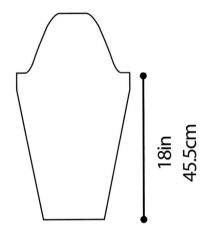

18in
45.5cm

PULLOVER

BACK

Using smaller needles cast on 162 (170, 178, 186, 198, 206) sts.

Row 1 (RS): K2, *P2, K2, rep from * to end.

Row 2: P2, *K2, P2, rep from * to end.

The last 2 rows form ribbing.

Work 18 rows more in ribbing, dec 2 (2, 0, 0, 2, 2) sts evenly across last row and ending with RS facing for next row—160 (168, 178, 186, 196, 204) sts.

Change to larger needles.

Row 1 (RS): P0 (0, 1, 1, 0, 0), [K1, P1] 2 (4, 6, 8, 11, 13) times, K1 tbl, work Row 1 of chart for Back and Front over next 150 sts, K1 tbl, [P1, K1] 2 (4, 6, 8, 11, 13) times, P0 (0, 1, 1, 0, 0).

Row 2: P0 (0, 1, 1, 0, 0), [K1, P1] 2 (4, 6, 8, 11, 13) times, P1 tbl, work Row 2 of chart for Back and Front over next 150 sts, P1 tbl, [P1, K1] 2 (4, 6, 8, 11, 13) times, P0 (0, 1, 1, 0, 0).

The last 2 rows place chart and seed st at side edges.

Work even as set, working appropriate rows of chart until back measures 18 (18½, 18, 18½, 18, 18½)in/ 45.5 (47, 45.5, 47, 45.5, 47)cm, ending with RS facing for next row.

Shape armholes

Keeping patt correct, bind off 2 (3, 4, 5, 6, 7) sts at beg of next 2 rows—156 (162, 170, 176, 184, 190) sts.

Dec 1 st at each end of next row, then every other row 2 (4, 5, 7, 9, 9) times—150 (152, 158, 160, 164, 170) sts. **

Work even until armhole measures 8½ (9, 9½, 10, 10½, 10¾)in/21.5 (23, 24, 25.5, 26.5, 27.5)cm, ending with RS facing for next row.

Shape shoulders and back neck

Keeping patt correct, bind off 14 (15, 15, 15, 15, 16) sts at beg of next 2 rows—122 (122, 128, 130, 134, 138) sts.

Next row (RS): Bind off 15 (15, 15, 16, 16, 17) sts in patt, work in patt until there are 19 (19, 20, 20, 20, 21) sts on right-hand needle, place rem sts on a st holder. Turn.

Work each side of neck separately.

Next row: Bind off 4 sts in patt, work in patt to end.

Bind off rem 15 (15, 16, 16, 16, 17) sts in patt.

Place rem sts on needle. With RS facing, rejoin yarn, bind off center 54 (54, 58, 58, 62, 62) sts, work in patt to end.

Complete to match first side, reversing shapings.

FRONT

Work as given for back to **.

Work even in patt until 16 (16, 18, 18, 20, 20) rows less than back to start of shoulder shaping, ending with RS facing for next row.

Divide for neck

Next row (RS): Patt 52 (53, 56, 57, 59, 62) sts, place rem sts on a st holder. Turn.

Work each side of neck separately.

Dec 1 st at neck edge on next 4 (4, 6, 6, 8, 8) rows, then on every other row 3 times, then foll 4th row once—44 (45, 46, 47, 47, 50) sts.

Work 1 row in patt, ending with RS facing for next row.

Shape Shoulder

Keeping patt correct, bind off 14 (15, 15, 15, 15, 16) sts at beg of next row and 15 (15, 15, 16, 16, 17) sts at beg of foll RS row.

Work 1 row in patt.

Bind off rem 15 (15, 16, 16, 16, 17) sts in patt.

Place rem sts on needle. With RS facing, rejoin yarn to rem sts, bind off center 46 sts, work in patt to end.

Complete to match first side, reversing shapings.

SLEEVES (Make 2)

Using smaller needles cast on 66 (70, 74, 74, 78, 82) sts.

Row 1 (RS): K2, *P2, K2, rep from * to end.

Row 2: P2, *K2, P2, rep from * to end.

The last 2 rows form ribbing.

Work 18 rows more in ribbing, dec 0 (2, 2, 0, 0, 2) sts evenly across last row and ending with RS facing for next row—66 (68, 72, 74, 78, 80) sts.

Change to larger needles.

Row 1 (RS): P0 (1, 1, 0, 0, 1), [K1, P1] 3 (3, 4, 5, 6, 6) times, K1 tbl, work Row 1 of Sleeve chart over next 52 sts, K1 tbl, [P1, K1] 3 (3, 4, 5, 6, 6) times, P0 (1, 1, 0, 0, 1).

Row 2: P0 (1, 1, 0, 0, 1), [K1, P1] 3 (3, 4, 5, 6, 6) times, P1 tbl, work Row 2 of Sleeve chart over next 52 sts, P1 tbl, [P1, K1] 3 (3, 4, 5, 6, 6) times, P0 (1, 1, 0, 0, 1).

The last 2 rows place chart and seed st at side edges.

Work in patt as set, working appropriate rows of chart and AT THE SAME TIME inc 1 st at each end of 5th row, then every 4th row until there are 88 (86, 90, 90, 92, 92) sts, then every 6th row until there are 108 (110, 114, 116, 120, 122) sts, working inc sts in patt.

Work even until sleeve measures 20 (20½, 21, 21¼, 21½, 22)in/51 (52, 53.5, 54, 54.5, 56)cm, ending with RS facing for next row.

Shape Top

Keeping patt correct, bind off 2 (3, 4, 5, 6, 7) sts at beg of next 2 rows—104 (104, 106, 106, 108, 108) sts.

Dec 1 st at each end of every other row 5 times, then dec 1 st at each end of next row—92 (92, 94, 94, 96, 96) sts.

Bind off rem 92 (92, 94, 94, 96, 96) sts.

NECKBAND

Join right shoulder seam.

With RS facing and using smaller needles, pick up and K20 (20, 21, 21, 22, 22) sts down left side of neck, 28 sts from front, 20 (20, 21, 21, 22, 22) sts up right side of neck and 46 (46, 48, 48, 50, 50) sts from back—114 (114, 118, 118, 122, 122) sts.

Row 1 (WS): P2, *K2, P2, rep from * to end.

Row 2: K2, *P2, K2, rep from * to end.

The last 2 rows form ribbing.

Work 5 more rows in ribbing, ending with RS facing for next row.

Bind off in ribbing.

FINISHING

Join left shoulder seam and neckband seam.

Sew in sleeves.

Sew side and sleeve seams.

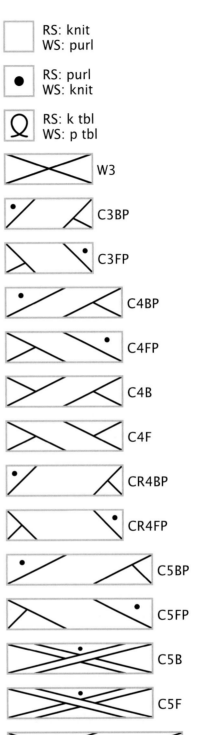

KEY

RS: knit
WS: purl

RS: purl
WS: knit

RS: k tbl
WS: p tbl

W3

C3BP

C3FP

C4BP

C4FP

C4B

C4F

CR4BP

CR4FP

C5BP

C5FP

C5B

C5F

C6B

C6F

Red border indicates rep

MEN'S CREWNECK PULLOVER BACK AND FRONT CHART

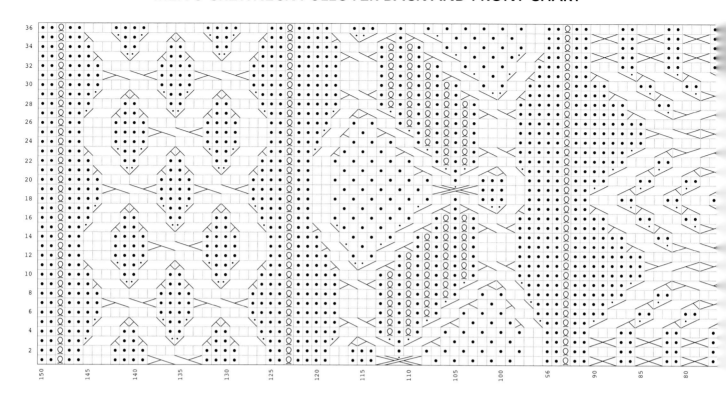

MEN'S CREWNECK PULLOVER SLEEVE CHART

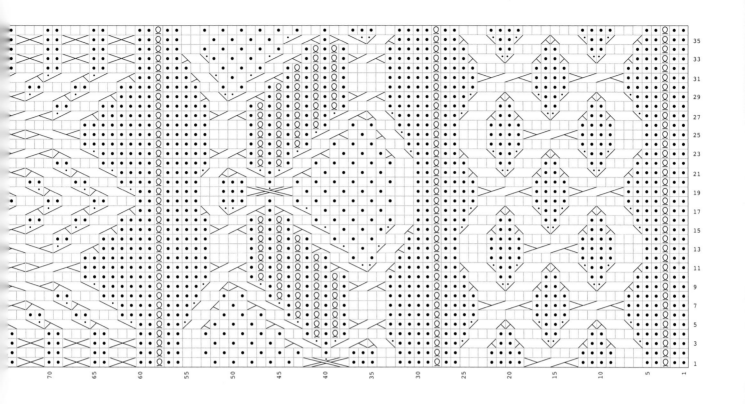

35
33
31
29
27
25
23
21
19
17
15
13
11
9
7
5
3
1

70   65   60   55   50   45   40   35   30   25   20   15   10   5   1

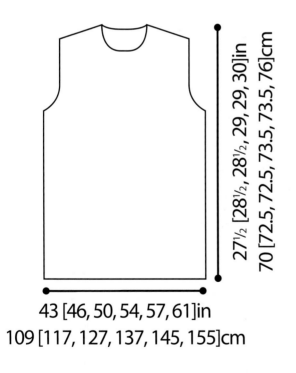

27½ [28½, 28½, 29, 29, 30]in
70 [72.5, 72.5, 73.5, 73.5, 76]cm

43 [46, 50, 54, 57, 61]in
109 [117, 127, 137, 145, 155]cm

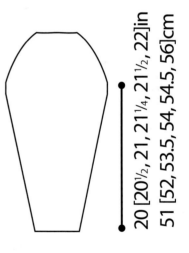

20 [20½, 21, 21¼, 21½, 22]in
51 [52, 53.5, 54, 54.5, 56]cm

CROSSOVER SHRUG

Skill Level ★

MEASUREMENTS AND YARN

Size	32–38 81.5–96.5	40–46 101.5–117	in cm
Width	12 30.5	12 30.5	in cm
Rowan Brushed Fleece (65% wool, 30% alpaca, 5% polyamide) in #254 Tarn	10	12	1¾oz/50g 115yds/105m hanks

OTHER MATERIALS

• 1 pair US 10½ (7mm) knitting needles OR SIZE TO OBTAIN GAUGE

• 2 spare knitting needles

• Cable needle

• Waste yarn

Gauge: 14 sts and 16 rows = 4in/10cm over St st using US 10½ (7mm) needles.

TAKE TIME TO CHECK GAUGE.

SPECIAL ABBREVIATIONS

C8B: Slip next 4 sts onto a cable needle and hold at back, K4, then K4 from cable needle.

C8F: Slip next 4 sts onto a cable needleand hold at front, K4, then K4 from cable needle.

C12B: Slip next 6 sts onto a cable needleand hold at back, K6, then K6 from cable needle.

C12F: Slip next 6 sts onto a cable needleand hold at front, K6, then K6 from cable needle.

SHRUG

FIRST LOOP

Using waste yarn cast on 64 sts.

Row 1 (WS): Purl.

Break off waste yarn and join in main yarn.

Working from chart A, rep the 8-row patt until work measures 49¼ (59)in/125 (150)cm, ending with RS facing for next row.

Unravel waste yarn and slip the 64 sts of the first row in main yarn onto a spare needle.

Holding both sets of 64 sts tog with RS facing each other (and ensuring strip is not twisted), bind off both sets of sts tog as if to knit, taking one st from front needle tog with corresponding st from back needle.

SECOND LOOP

Using waste yarn cast on 58 sts.

Row 1 (WS): Purl.

Break off waste yarn and join in main yarn.

Working from chart B, rep the 12-row patt until second loop measures same as first loop, ending with RS facing for next row.

Unravel waste yarn and slip the 58 sts of the first row in main yarn onto a spare needle.

Slip one end of this loop through center of first loop (so resulting joined loops will be interlocked) and, holding both sets of 58 sts tog with RS facing each other (and ensuring strip is not twisted), bind off both sets of sts tog as if to knit, taking one st from front needle tog with corresponding st from back needle.

FINISHING

Sew in all loose ends.

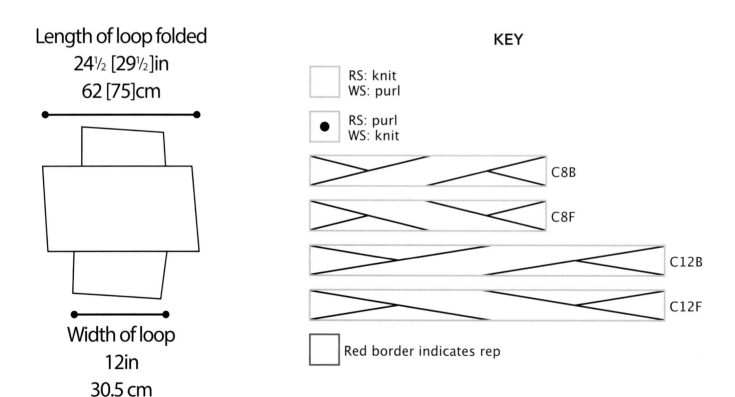

Length of loop folded
24½ [29½]in
62 [75]cm

Width of loop
12in
30.5 cm

KEY

RS: knit
WS: purl

RS: purl
WS: knit

C8B

C8F

C12B

C12F

Red border indicates rep

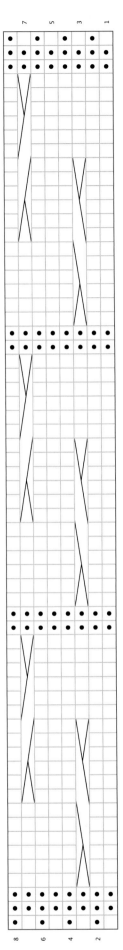

CROSSOVER SHRUG CHART A

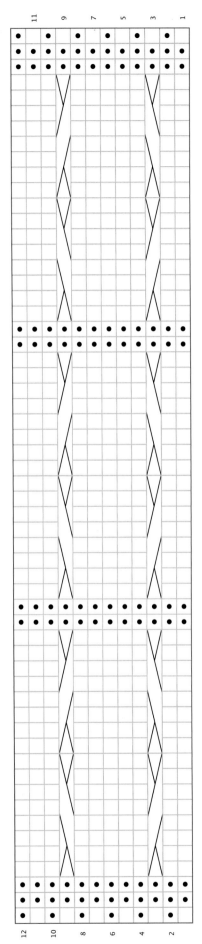

CROSSOVER SHRUG CHART B

MEN'S SHAWL COLLAR PULLOVER

Skill Level ★★

MEASUREMENTS AND YARN

To fit chest	40 101.5	42 106.5	44 112	46 117	48 122	50 127	in cm
Actual size	45 114	48 122	50 127	52 132	55 140	57 145	in cm
Full Length (approximately)	26¾ 68	27¾ 70.5	27½ 70	28½ 72.5	28½ 72.5	29¼ 74.5	in cm
Sleeve Length (adjustable)	20 51	20½ 52	21 53.5	21½ 54.5	22 56	22½ 57	in cm
Rowan All Seasons Cotton (60% cotton, 40% acrylic) in #249 Denim	24	25	26	27	28	29	1¾oz/50g 98yds/90m balls

OTHER MATERIALS

• 1 pair US 6 (4mm) knitting needles OR SIZE TO OBTAIN GAUGE

• 1 pair US 8 (5mm) knitting needles OR SIZE TO OBTAIN GAUGE

• 1 US 6 (4mm) 60cm circular needle OR SIZE TO OBTAIN GAUGE

• Cable needle

Gauge: 27 sts and 24 rows = 4in/10cm in patt using US 8 (5mm) needles.

TAKE TIME TO CHECK GAUGE.

SPECIAL ABBREVIATIONS

C4BP: Slip next st onto a cable needle and hold at back, K3, then P1 from cable needle.

C4FP: Slip next 3 sts onto a cable needle and hold at front, P1, then K3 from cable needle.

C5BP: Slip next 2 sts onto a cable needle and hold at back, K3, then P2 from cable needle.

C5FP: Slip next 3 sts onto a cable needle and hold at front, P2, then K3 from cable needle.

C6F: Slip next 3 sts onto a cable needle and hold at front, K3, then K3 from cable needle.

PULLOVER

BACK

Using smaller needles cast on 154 (162, 170, 178, 186, 194) sts.

Row 1 (RS): K2, *P2, K2, rep from * to end.

Row 2: P2, *K2, P2, rep from * to end.

The last 2 rows form ribbing.

Work 20 rows more in ribbing, ending with RS facing for next row.

Change to larger needles.

Row 1 (RS): K9 (13, 17, 21, 5, 9), [work Row 1 of chart over next 16 sts, K4] 6 (6, 6, 6, 8, 8) times, work Row 1 of chart over next 16 sts, K9 (13, 17, 21, 5, 9).

Row 2: P9 (13, 17, 21, 5, 9), [work Row 2 of chart over next 16 sts, P4] 6 (6, 6, 6, 8, 8) times, work Row 2 of chart over next 16 sts, P9 (13, 17, 21, 5, 9).

The last 2 rows set position of cable panel and St st sections.

Work even as set working appropriate row of chart until back measures 17 (17½, 17, 17½, 17, 17½)in/43 (44.5, 43, 44.5, 43, 44.5)cm, ending with RS facing for next row.

Shape armholes

Keeping patt correct, bind off 3 (4, 4, 5, 5, 5) sts at beg of next 2 rows—148 (154, 162, 168, 176, 184) sts. **

Dec 1 st at each end of next 1 (1, 3, 3, 3, 3) rows, then every other row 3 (3, 2, 2, 3, 3) times—140 (146, 152, 158, 164, 172) sts.

Work even until armhole measures 9 (9½, 9¾, 10¼, 10¾, 11)in/23 (24, 25, 26, 27.5, 28)cm, ending with RS facing for next row.

Shape shoulders and back neck

Keeping patt correct, bind off 14 (15, 16, 17, 17, 19) sts at beg of next 2 rows—112 (116, 120, 124, 130, 134) sts.

Next row (RS): Bind off 14 (15, 16, 17, 17, 19) sts, work in patt until there are 18 (19, 19, 20, 22, 22) sts on needle, place rem sts on a holder, turn.

Work each side of neck separately.

Next row: Bind off 4 sts, work in patt to end—14 (15, 15, 16, 18, 18) sts.

Bind off rem sts.

With RS facing, place sts from holder on needle. Rejoin yarn, bind off center 48 (48, 50, 50, 52, 52) sts, work in patt to end.

Complete to match first side of neck, reversing all shapings.

FRONT

Work as given for back to **.

Dec 1 st at each end of next 1 (1, 3, 3, 3, 3) rows—146 (152, 156, 162, 170, 178) sts.

Work 1 row even in patt, ending with RS facing for next row.

Shape front neck

Next row (RS): Patt2tog, work 59 (62, 64, 67, 71, 75) sts in patt, place rem sts on holder, turn.

Work each side of neck separately.

Work 1 row even in patt.

Dec 1 st at each end of next row, then on 1 (1, 0, 0, 1, 1) foll RS row—55 (58, 62, 65, 69, 71) sts.

Dec 1 st at neck edge only on every other row 9 (8, 10, 9, 9, 8) times, then on every 4th row until 42 (45, 47, 50, 52, 56) sts rem.

Work even until armhole matches back to start of shoulder shaping, ending with RS facing for next row.

Shape shoulder

Keeping patt correct, bind off 14 (15, 16, 17, 17, 19) sts at beg of next row—29 (30, 31, 33, 35, 37) sts.

Work 1 row in patt.

Bind off 14 (15, 16, 17, 17, 19) sts at beg of next row—14 (15, 15, 16, 18, 18) sts.

Work 1 row in patt.

Bind off rem sts.

With RS facing, place sts from holder on needle, bind off center 24 sts, work in patt to last 2 sts, patt2tog.

Complete to match first side of neck, reversing all shapings.

SLEEVES (Make 2)

Using smaller needles cast on 66 (66, 70, 70, 74, 74) sts.

Row 1 (RS): K2, *P2, K2, rep from * to end.

Row 2: P2, *K2, P2, rep from * to end.

The last 2 rows form ribbing.

Work 20 rows more in ribbing, ending with RS facing for next row.

Change to larger needles.

Row 1 (RS): K5 (5, 7, 7, 9, 9), [work Row 1 of chart across next 16 sts, K4] 3 times, K1 (1, 3, 3, 5, 5).

Row 2: P5 (5, 7, 7, 9, 9), [work Row 2 of chart over next 16 sts, P4] 3 times, P1 (1, 3, 3, 5, 5).

The last 2 rows set position of cable panel and St st sections.

Work in patt as set, working appropriate row of chart and AT THE SAME TIME inc 1 st at each end of 3rd row, then every 4th row until there are 76 (76, 80, 80, 82, 84) sts, then on every 6th row until there are 100 (102, 104, 106, 108, 110) sts.

Work even until sleeve measures 20 (20½, 21, 21½, 22, 22½)in/51 (52, 53.5, 54.5, 56, 57)cm, ending with RS facing for next row.

Shape sleeve top

Keeping patt correct, bind off 3 (4, 4, 5, 5, 5) sts at beg of next 2 rows—94 (94, 96, 96, 98, 100) sts.

Dec 1 st at each end of next 1 (1, 3, 3, 3, 3) rows, then on every other row, 3 (3, 2, 2, 3, 3) times, then on foll row once—84 (84, 84, 84, 84, 86) sts.

Bind off.

SHAWL COLLAR

Join both shoulder seams.

With RS facing, using circular needle, pick up and K44 (46, 49, 51, 52, 54) sts up right side of neck, 38 (38, 40, 40, 42, 42) sts across back neck and 44 (46, 49, 51, 52, 54) sts down left side of neck—126 (130, 138, 142, 146, 150) sts.

Next row (WS): P2, *K2, P2, rep from * to end.

Next row: K2, *P2, K2, rep from * to end.

The last 2 rows form ribbing.

Rows 3–11: Work in ribbing, ending with RS facing for next row.

Row 12 (RS): Rib 82 (84, 89, 91, 94, 96), wrap next st by slipping next st from left-hand needle to right-hand needle, taking yarn to opposite side of work between needles and then slipping same st back to left-hand needle, turn. When working back across wrapped sts, work the wrapped st and the wrapped loop tog as one st, turn.

Row 13: Rib 38 (38, 41, 41, 42, 42), wrap next st and turn.

Row 14: Rib 40 (40, 43, 43; 44, 44), wrap next st and turn.

Row 15: Rib 42 (42, 45, 45, 46, 46), wrap next st and turn.

Cont in this way working an extra 2 sts on every row before wrapping st until the following row has been worked.

Row 51: Rib 114 (114, 117, 117, 118, 118) sts, wrap next st and turn.

Row 52: Rib to end.

Work 11 rows more in rib.

Bind off loosely in rib.

FINISHING

Sew row ends of left shawl collar in place to bound-off sts at front neck; place row ends of right side of shawl collar behind left side of shawl collar and sew in place.

Fold sleeve in half lengthways, placing fold to shoulder seam, sew in sleeves.

Join side and sleeve seams.

KEY

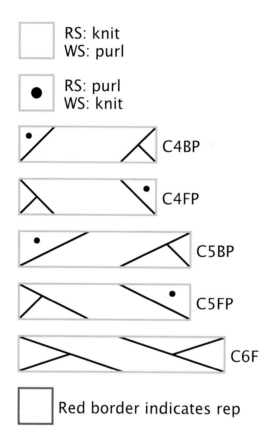

RS: knit
WS: purl

RS: purl
WS: knit

C4BP

C4FP

C5BP

C5FP

C6F

Red border indicates rep

MEN'S SHAWL COLLAR PULLOVER CHART

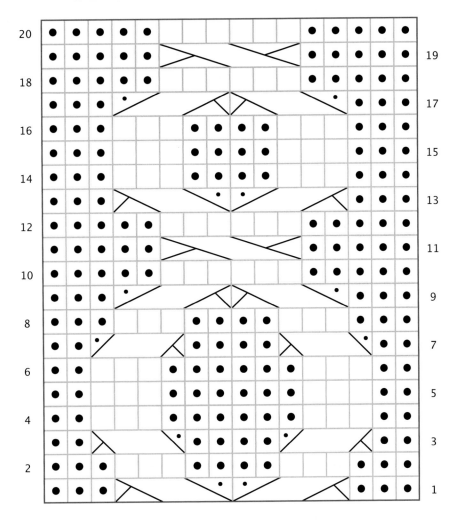

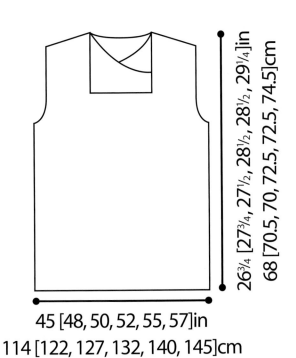

26¾ [27¾, 27½, 28½, 28½, 29¼]in
68 [70.5, 70, 72.5, 72.5, 74.5]cm

45 [48, 50, 52, 55, 57]in
114 [122, 127, 132, 140, 145]cm

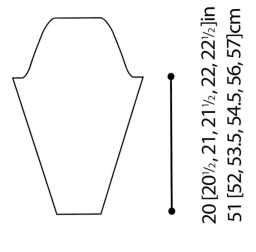

20 [20½, 21, 21½, 22, 22½]in
51 [52, 53.5, 54.5, 56, 57]cm

BUTTONLESS CHUNKY CARDIGAN

Skill Level ★★★

MEASUREMENTS AND YARN

To fit bust	32–34 81.5–86.5	34–36 86.5–91.5	36–38 91.5–96.5	38–40 96.5–101.5	40–42 101.5–106.5	42–44 106.5–112	in cm
Actual size	41 104	43 109	44½ 113	46½ 118	48 122	50 127	in cm
Full Length (approximately)	30¼ 77	31½ 80	32¾ 83	34¼ 87	34¾ 88.5	35½ 90	in cm
Sleeve Length (adjustable)	11 28	11 28	12½ 32	12 30.5	11¾ 30	11¾ 30	in cm
Cascade® Lana Grande (100% Peruvian Highland wool) in # 6073 Basil	9	10	12	13	14	15	3½oz/100g 87.5yds/80m balls

OTHER MATERIALS

• 1 pair US 13 (9mm) knitting needles OR SIZE TO OBTAIN GAUGE

• 1 pair US 15 (10mm) knitting needles OR SIZE TO OBTAIN GAUGE

• Stitch holders

• Stitch markers

• Cable needle

Gauge: 9 sts and 12 rows = 4in/10cm in St st using US 15 (10mm) needles.

TAKE TIME TO CHECK GAUGE.

SPECIAL ABBREVIATIONS

C3B: Slip next st onto a cable needle and hold at back, K2, then K1 from cable needle.

C3F: Slip next 2 sts onto a cable needle and hold at front, K1, then K2 from cable needle.

C3BP: Slip next st onto a cable needle and hold at back, K2, then P1 from cable needle.

C3FP: Slip next 2 sts onto a cable needle and hold at front, P1, then K2 from cable needle.

C5B: Slip next 3 sts onto a cable needle and hold at back, K2, then K3 from cable needle.

CARDIGAN
BACK

Using smaller needles cast on 58 (58, 62, 62, 66, 66) sts.

Row 1 (RS): K2, *P2, K2, rep from * to end.

Row 2: P2, *K2, P2, rep from * to end.

The last 2 rows form ribbing.

Work 4 more rows in ribbing, dec (inc, dec, inc, dec, inc) 1 st at center of last row, ending with RS facing for next row—57 (59, 61, 63, 65, 67) sts.

Change to larger needles.

Row 1 (RS): P2 (3, 1, 2, 3, 4), *K2, P2 (2, 3, 3, 3, 3), work Row 1 of chart over next 11 sts, P2 (2, 3, 3, 3, 3), rep from * twice more, K2, P2 (3, 1, 2, 3, 4).

Row 2: K2 (3, 1, 2, 3, 4), *P2, K2 (2, 3, 3, 3, 3), work Row 2 of chart over next 11 sts, K2 (2, 3, 3, 3, 3), rep from * twice more, P2, K2 (3, 1, 2, 3, 4).

The last 2 rows set patt and chart.

Cont working appropriate rows of chart for 46 (48, 50, 52, 54, 56) more rows, ending with Row 16 (2, 4, 6, 8, 10) of chart and RS facing for next row.

Shape sleeves

For 1st size only

Next row (RS): Cast on 30 sts, work across these sts as follows: P2, work Row 1 of chart over next 11 sts, P2, K2, P2, work Row 1 of chart over next 11 sts, work in patt to end.

Next row: Cast on 30 sts, work across these sts as follows: K2, work Row 2 of chart over next 11 sts, K2, P2, K2, work Row 2 of chart over next 11 sts, work in patt to end—117 sts.

For 2nd size only

Next row (RS): Cast on 29 sts, work across these sts as follows: P2, work Row 3 of chart over next 11 sts, P2, K2, P2, work Row 3 of chart over next 10 sts of sleeve and first st of body, work in patt to end.

Next row: Cast on 29 sts, work across these sts as follows: K2, work Row 4 of chart over next 11 sts, K2, P2, K2, work Row 4 of chart over next 10 sts of sleeve and first st of body, work in patt to end—117 sts.

For 3rd size only

Next row (RS): Cast on 34 sts, work across these sts as follows: P2, work Row 5 of chart over next 11 sts, P3, K2, P3, work Row 5 of chart over next 11 sts, P2, work in patt to end.

Next row: Cast on 34 sts, work across these sts as follows: K2, work Row 6 of chart over next 11 sts, K3, P2, K3, work Row 6 of chart over next 11 sts, K2, work in patt to end—129 sts.

For 4th size only

Next row (RS): Cast on 33 sts, work across these sts as follows: P2, work Row 7 of chart over next 11 sts, P3, K2, P3, work Row 7 of chart over next 11 sts, P1, work in patt to end.

Next row: Cast on 33 sts, work across these sts as follows: K2, work Row 8 of chart over next 11 sts, K3, P2, K3, work Row 8 of chart over next 11 sts, K1, work in patt to end—129 sts.

For 5th size only

Next row (RS): Cast on 32 sts, work across these sts as follows: P2, work Row 9 of chart over next 11 sts, P3, K2, P3, work Row 9 of chart over next 11 sts, work in patt to end.

Next row: Cast on 32 sts, work across these sts as follows: K2, work Row 10 of chart over next 11 sts, K3, P2, K3, work Row 10 of chart over next 11 sts, work in patt to end—129 sts.

For 6th size only

Next row (RS): Cast on 31 sts, work across these sts as follows: P2, work Row 11 of chart over next 11 sts, P3, K2, P3, work Row 11 of chart over next 10 sts of sleeve and first st of body, work in patt to end.

Next row: Cast on 31 sts, work across these sts as follows: K2, work Row 12 of chart over next 11 sts, K3, P2, K3, work Row 12 of chart over next 10 sts of sleeve and first st of body, work in patt to end—129 sts.

For all sizes

Working all sts in patt as set by last 2 rows, work even in patt for 26 (28, 30, 32, 32, 34) more rows, ending with Row 12 (16, 4, 8, 10, 14) of chart and RS facing for next row.

Shape overarm and shoulders

Keeping patt correct, bind off 8 (8, 9, 9, 9, 8) sts at beg of next 10 (12, 12, 12, 12, 2) rows, then 9 (0, 0, 0, 0, 9) sts at beg of next 2 (0, 0, 0, 0, 10) rows, ending with RS facing for next row.

Bind off rem 19 (21, 21, 21, 21, 23) sts.

LEFT FRONT

Using smaller needles cast on 23 (27, 27, 27, 27, 31) sts.

Row 1 (RS): *K2, P2, rep from * to last 3 sts, K3.

Row 2: K1, P2, *K2, P2, rep from * to end.

The last 2 rows form ribbing.

Work 4 more rows in ribbing, inc (dec, dec, 0, inc, dec) 1 (2, 1, 0, 1, 2) sts evenly across last row, ending with RS facing for next row—24 (25, 26, 27, 28, 29) sts.

Change to larger needles.

Row 1 (RS): P2 (3, 1, 2, 3, 4), K2, P2 (2, 3, 3, 3, 3), work Row 1 of chart over next 11 sts, P2 (2, 3, 3, 3, 3), K2, P3 (3, 4, 4, 4, 4).

Row 2: K3 (3, 4, 4, 4, 4), P2, K2 (2, 3, 3, 3, 3), work Row 2 of chart over next 11 sts, K2 (2, 3, 3, 3, 3), P2, K2 (3, 1, 2, 3, 4).

The last 2 rows set patt and chart.

Cont working appropriate rows of chart for 46 (48, 50, 52, 54, 56) more rows, ending with Row 16 (2, 4, 6, 8, 10) of chart and RS facing for next row.

Shape sleeve and front slope

For 1st size only

Next row (RS): Cast on 30 sts, work across these sts as follows: P2, work Row 1 of chart over next 11 sts, P2, K2, P2, work Row 1 of chart over next 11 sts, work in patt to last 2 sts, patt2tog—53 sts.

For 2nd size only

Next row (RS): Cast on 29 sts, work across these sts as follows: P2, work Row 3 of chart over next 11 sts, P2, K2, P2, work Row 3 of chart over next 10 sts of sleeve and first st of body, work in patt to last 2 sts, patt2tog—53 sts.

For 3rd size only

Next row (RS): Cast on 34 sts, work across these sts as follows: P2, work Row 5 of chart over next 11 sts, P3, K2, P3, work Row 5 of chart over next 11 sts, P2, work in patt to last 2 sts, patt2tog—59 sts.

For 4th size only

Next row (RS): Cast on 33 sts, work across these sts as follows: P2, work Row 7 of chart over next 11 sts, P3, K2, P3, work Row 7 of chart over next 11 sts, P1, patt to last 2 sts, patt2tog—59 sts.

For 5th size only

Next row (RS): Cast on 32 sts, work across these sts as follows: P2, work Row 9 of chart over next 11 sts, P3, K2, P3, work Row 9 of chart over next 11 sts, work in patt to last 2 sts, patt2tog—59 sts.

For 6th size only

Next row (RS): Cast on 31 sts, work across these sts as follows: P2, work Row 11 of chart over next 11 sts, P3, K2, P3, work Row 11 of chart over next 10 sts of sleeve and first st of body, work in patt to last 2 sts, patt2tog—59 sts.

For all sizes

Working all sts in patt as set by last row, cont in patt for 27 (29, 31, 33, 33, 35) more rows, dec 1 st at front slope edge every 6th row 4 (4, 5, 5, 5, 5) times, then every 4th row 0(1, 0, 0, 0, 1) time, ending with Row 12 (16, 4, 7, 10, 14 of chart and RS facing for next row—49 (48, 54, 54, 54, 53) sts.

Shape overarm and shoulders

Keeping patt correct, bind off 8 (8, 9, 9, 9, 8) sts at side edge 5(6, 6, 6, 6, 1) times, then 9 (0, 0, 0, 0, 9) sts 1 (0, 0, 0, 0, 5) times.

RIGHT FRONT

Using smaller needles cast on 23 (27, 27, 27, 27, 31) sts.

Row 1 (RS): K3, *P2, K2 rep from * to end.

Row 2: *P2, K2, rep from * to last 3 sts, P2, K1.

The last 2 rows form ribbing.

Work 4 more rows in ribbing, inc (dec, dec, 0, inc, dec) 1 (2, 1, 0, 1, 2) sts evenly across last row, ending with RS facing for next row—24 (25, 26, 27, 28, 29) sts.

Change to larger needles.

Row 1 (RS): P3 (3, 4. 4, 4, 4), K2, P2 (2, 3, 3, 3, 3), work Row 1 of chart over next 11 sts, P2 (2, 3, 3, 3, 3), K2, P2 (3, 1, 2, 3, 4)

Row 2: K2 (3, 1, 2, 3, 4), P2, K2 (2, 3, 3, 3, 3), work Row 2 of chart over next 11 sts, K2 (2, 3, 3, 3, 3), P2, K3 (3, 4, 4, 4, 4).

The last 2 rows set patt and chart.

Cont working appropriate rows of chart for 46 (48, 50, 52, 54, 56) more rows, ending with Row 16 (2, 4, 6, 8, 10) of chart and RS facing for next row.

Next row (RS): Patt2tog, work in patt to end—23 (24, 25, 26, 27, 28) sts.

Shape sleeve and front slope

For 1st size only

Next row (WS): Cast on 30 sts, work across these sts as follows: K2, work Row 2 of chart over next 11 sts, K2, P2, K2, work Row 2 of chart over next 11 sts, patt to end—53 sts.

For 2nd size only

Next row (WS): Cast on 29 sts, work across these sts as follows: K2, work Row 4 of chart over next 11 sts, K2, P2, K2, work Row 4 of chart over next 10 sts of sleeve and first st of body, work in patt to end—53 sts.

For 3rd size only

Next row (WS): Cast on 34 sts, work across these sts as follows, K2, work Row 6 of chart over next 11 sts, K3, P2, K3, work Row 6 of chart over next 11 sts, K2, work in patt to end—59 sts.

For 4th size only

Next row (WS): Cast on 33 sts, work across these sts as follows: K2, work Row 8 of chart over next 11 sts, K3, P2, K3, work Row 8 of chart over next 11 sts, K1, work in patt to end—59 sts.

For 5th size only

Next row (WS): Cast on 32 sts, work across these sts as follows: K2, work Row 10 of chart over next 11 sts, K3, P2, K3, work Row 10 of chart over next 11 sts, work in patt to end—59 sts.

For 6th size only

Next row (WS): Cast on 31 sts, work across these sts as follows: K2, work Row 12 of chart over next 11 sts, K3, P2, K3, work Row 12 of chart over next 10 sts of sleeve and first st of body, work in patt to end—59 sts.

For all sizes

Working all sts in patt as set by last row, work in patt for 27 (29, 31, 33, 33, 35) more rows, dec 1 st at front slope edge on 5th, then every 6th row 3 (3, 4, 4, 4, 4) times, then every 4th row 0 (1, 0, 0, 0, 1) time, ending with Row 13 (1, 5, 9, 11, 15) of chart and WS facing for next row—49 (48, 54, 54, 54, 53) sts.

Shape overarm and shoulders

Keeping patt correct, bind off 8 (8, 9, 9, 9, 8) sts at side edge 5(6, 6, 6, 6, 1) times, then 9 (0, 0, 0, 0, 9) sts 1 (0, 0, 0, 0, 5) time.

RIGHT FRONT BORDER

Join shoulder and overarm seams.

With RS facing, using smaller needles, starting from cast-on edge, pick up and K47 (49, 51, 53, 55, 57) sts evenly along right front opening edge to start of front slope shaping, 28 (30, 31, 33, 35, 36) sts up right front slope to shoulder, then 8 (8, 9, 9, 9, 10) sts across to center back neck—83 (87, 91, 95, 99, 103) sts.

Row 1 (WS): *P2, K2, rep from * to last 3 sts, P2, K1.

Row 2: K3, *P2, K2, rep from * to end.

The last 2 rows form ribbing.

Work 4 more rows in ribbing, ending with WS facing for next row.

Bind off in ribbing.

LEFT FRONT BORDER

With RS facing, using US 13 (9mm) needles, starting from center back neck, pick up and K8 (8, 9, 9, 9, 10) sts across back neck, 28 (30, 31, 33, 35, 36) sts down left front slope to shoulder, then 47 (49, 51, 53, 55, 57) sts evenly along left front opening edge to cast-on edge—83 (87, 91, 95, 99, 103) sts.

Row 1 (WS): K1, P2, *P2, K2, rep from * to end.

Row 2: *P2, K2, rep from * to last 3 sts, K3.

The last 2 rows form ribbing.

Work 4 more rows in ribbing, ending with WS facing for next row.

Bind off in ribbing.

SLEEVE CUFFS

With RS facing, using smaller needles, pick up and K50 (54, 58, 58, 58, 62) sts evenly along row end edge of sleeve extension.

Row 1 (WS): P2, *K2, P2, rep from * to end.

Row 2: K2, *P2, K2, rep from * to end.

The last 2 rows form ribbing.

Work 2 more rows in ribbing, ending with WS facing for next row.

Bind off in ribbing.

FINISHING

Join side, sleeve, and sleeve cuff seams.

KEY

- ☐ RS: knit / WS: purl
- ⬛ RS: purl / WS: knit
- C3B
- C3F
- C3BP
- C3FP
- C5B
- ☐ Red border indicates rep

CHART

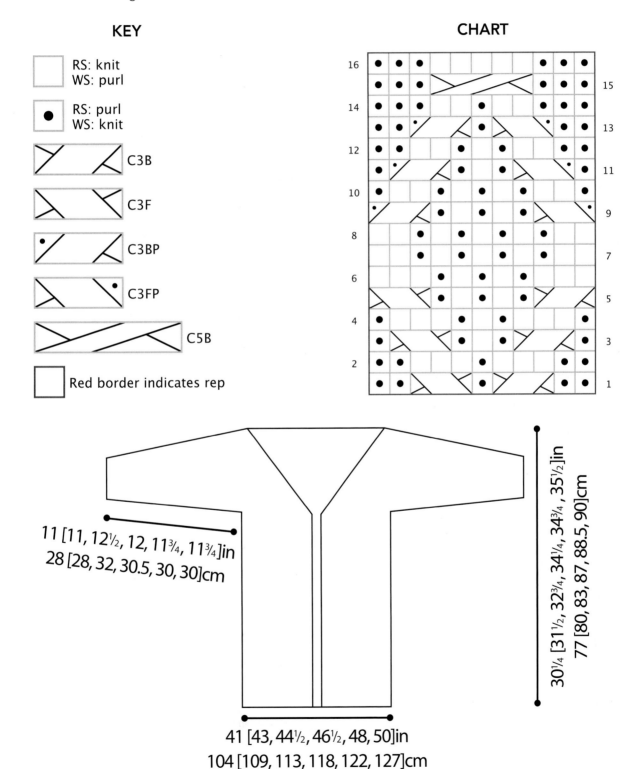

11 [11, 12½, 12, 11¾, 11¾]in
28 [28, 32, 30.5, 30, 30]cm

41 [43, 44½, 46½, 48, 50]in
104 [109, 113, 118, 122, 127]cm

30¼ [31½, 32¾, 34¼, 34¾, 35½]in
77 [80, 83, 87, 88.5, 90]cm

DIAMOND CABLED PULLOVER

Skill Level ★★

MEASUREMENTS AND YARN

To fit bust	32 81.5	34 86.5	36 91.5	38 96.5	40 101.5	42 106.5	44 112	in cm
Actual size	38½ 98	40½ 103	42½ 108	43½ 110.5	45½ 115.5	47½ 120.5	48 122	in cm
Full Length (approximately)	25½ 65	25½ 65	26 66	26 66	26½ 67.5	26½ 67.5	26½ 67.5	in cm
Sleeve Length (adjustable)	17½ 44.5	18 45.5	18 45.5	18 45.5	18 45.5	19 48.5	19 48.5	in cm
Drops Big Merino (100% merino wool) in #016 Light Pink	16	17	18	19	21	23	24	1¾oz/50g 82yds/75m balls

OTHER MATERIALS

• 1 pair US 6 (4mm) knitting needles OR SIZE TO OBTAIN GAUGE

• 1 pair US 8 (5mm) knitting needles OR SIZE TO OBTAIN GAUGE

• Cable needle

• Stitch holders

Gauge: 17 sts and 24 rows = 4in/10cm in St st using US 8 (5mm) needles.

TAKE TIME TO CHECK GAUGE.

SPECIAL ABBREVIATIONS

C4BK: Slip next st onto a cable needle and hold at back, K3, then K1 from cable needle.

C4FK: Slip next 3 sts onto a cable needle and hold at front, K1, then K3 from cable needle.

C4BP: Slip next st onto a cable needle and hold at back, K3, then P1 from cable needle.

C4FP: Slip next 3 sts onto a cable needle and hold at front, P1, then K3 from cable needle.

C5BP: Slip next 2 sts onto a cable needle and hold at back, K3, then P2 from cable needle.

C5FP: Slip next 3 sts onto a cable needle and hold at front, P2, then K3 from cable needle.

C6B: Slip next 3 sts onto a cable needle and hold at back, K3, then K3 from cable needle.

C6F: Slip next 3 sts onto a cable needle and hold at front, K3, then K3 from cable needle.

C8B: Slip next 4 sts onto a cable needle and hold at back, K4, then K4 from cable needle.

C8F: Slip next 4 sts onto a cable needle and hold at front, K4, then K4 from cable needle.

PULLOVER

BACK

Using smaller needles cast on 87 (91, 95, 99, 103, 107, 111) sts.

Row 1 (RS): K1, *P1, K1, rep from * to end.

Row 2: P1, *K1, P1, rep from * to end.

The last 2 rows form ribbing.

Work 11 more rows in ribbing, ending with WS facing for next row.

Row 14 (WS): Rib 2 (4, 6, 8, 6, 8, 10), *m1, rib 2, rep from * to last 3 (5, 7, 9, 7, 9, 11) sts, m1, rib to end—129 (133, 137, 141, 149, 153, 157) sts.

Change to larger needles.

Row 1 (RS): [P1, K1] 3 (4, 5, 6, 8, 9, 10) times, work Row 1 of chart A over next 117 sts, [K1, P1] 3 (4, 5, 6, 8, 9, 10) times.

Row 2: [K1, P1] 3 (4, 5, 6, 8, 9, 10) times, work Row 2 of chart A over next 117 sts, [P1, K1] 3 (4, 5, 6, 8, 9, 10) times.

Row 3: [K1, P1] 3 (4, 5, 6, 8, 9, 10) times, work Row 3 of chart A over next 117 sts, [P1, K1] 3 (4, 5, 6, 8, 9, 10) times.

Row 4: [P1, K1] 3 (4, 5, 6, 8, 9, 10) times, work Row 4 of chart A over next 117 sts, [K1, P1] 3 (4, 5, 6, 8, 9, 10) times.

The last 4 rows position chart and double seed st at either side.

Work even in patt as set, working appropriate rows of chart A for 82 (80, 78, 76, 76, 74, 70) more rows, ending with RS facing for next row. Place a marker at each end of last row to mark beg of armhole.

Shape armholes

Keeping patt correct, dec 1 st at each end of next 6 (6, 6, 8, 8, 8, 10) rows—117 (121, 125, 125, 133, 137, 137) sts. **

Work 42 (44, 48, 48, 52, 54, 56) rows even in patt.

Shape shoulders

Keeping patt correct, bind off 13 (14, 14, 14, 15, 16, 16) sts at beg of next 4 rows, then 14 (14, 15, 15, 16, 16, 16) sts at beg of foll 2 rows—37 (37, 39, 39, 41, 41, 41) sts.

Slip rem 37 (37, 39, 39, 41, 41, 41) sts onto a holder.

FRONT

Work as given for back to **.

Work 28 (30, 32, 32, 34, 36, 38) rows even in patt.

Shape neck

Next row (RS): Work in patt over 51 (53, 54, 54, 57, 59, 59) sts, place rem sts on a holder. Turn.

Work each side of the neck separately.

Keeping patt correct, bind off 3 sts at beg of next and foll WS row, 2 sts at beg of foll 2 WS rows, then dec 1 st at beg of foll WS row—40 (42, 43, 43, 46, 48, 48) sts.

Work 4 (4, 6, 6, 8, 8, 8) rows even in patt.

Shape shoulder

Keeping patt correct, bind off 13 (14, 14, 14, 15, 16, 16) sts at beg of next and foll RS row and 14 (14, 15, 15, 16, 16, 16) sts at beg of foll RS row.

Leave center 15 (15, 17, 17, 19, 19, 19) sts on holder. With RS facing, place rem sts on needle, rejoin yarn and work in patt to end—51 (53, 54, 54, 57, 59, 59) sts.

Next row (WS): Work even in patt.

Complete to match first side reversing shapings.

SLEEVES (Make 2)

Using smaller needles cast on 37 (39, 41, 43, 45, 49, 51) sts.

Row 1 (RS): K1, *P1, K1, rep from * to end.

Row 2: P1, *K1, P1, rep from * to end.

The last 2 rows form ribbing.

Work 11 more rows in ribbing, ending with WS facing for next row.

Row 14 (WS): Rib 5 (4, 3, 2, 1, 3, 2), *m1, rib 2, rep from * to last 6 (5, 4, 3, 2, 4, 3) sts, m1, rib to end—51 (55, 59, 63, 67, 71, 75) sts.

Change to larger needles.

Row 1 (RS): [P1, K1] 2 (3, 4, 5, 6, 7, 8) times, work Row 1 of chart B over next 43 sts, [K1, P1] 2 (3, 4, 5, 6, 7, 8) times.

Row 2: (K1, P1) 2 (3, 4, 5, 6, 7, 8) times, work Row 2 of chart B over next 43 sts, [P1, K1] 2 (3, 4, 5, 6, 7, 8) times.

Row 3: [K1, P1] 2 (3, 4, 5, 6, 7, 8) times, work Row 3 of chart B over next 43 sts, [P1, K1] 2 (3, 4, 5, 6, 7, 8) times.

Row 4: [P1, K1] 2 (3, 4, 5, 6, 7, 8) times, work Row 4 of chart B over next 43 sts, [K1, P1] 2 (3, 4, 5, 6, 7, 8) times.

The last 4 rows position chart and double seed st at either side.

Work in patt as set working appropriate rows of chart B. AT THE SAME TIME inc 1 st at each end of next and every foll 4th row, working extra sts in double seed st until 91 (95, 99, 103, 107, 113, 117) sts are on the needle.

Work 11 (13, 13, 13, 13, 15, 15) rows even in patt.

Place a marker at each end of last row to mark beg of shape top.

Shape top

Keeping patt correct, dec 1 st at each end of next 6 (6, 6, 8, 8, 8, 10) rows—79 (83, 87, 87, 91, 97, 97) sts.

Bind off in patt.

NECKBAND

Join right shoulder seam.

With RS facing and using smaller needles, pick up and K19 (19, 21, 21, 23, 23, 23) sts evenly down left side of front neck, K15 (15, 17, 17, 19, 19, 19) sts from front neck st holder, pick up and K20 (20, 22, 22, 24, 24, 24) sts evenly up right side of front neck and K37 (37, 39, 39, 41, 41, 41) sts from back neck st holder—91 (91, 99, 99, 107, 107, 107) sts.

Row 1 (WS): P1, *K1, P1, rep from * to end.

Row 2: K1, *P1, K1, rep from * to end.

The last 2 rows form ribbing.

Work 7 more rows in ribbing, ending with RS facing for next row.

Bind off loosely in rib.

FINISHING

Join left shoulder and neckband seam. Place center of bound-off edge of sleeves to shoulder seams, then sew in sleeves evenly to back and front, matching markers. Join side and sleeve seams.

DIAMOND CABLED PULLOVER CHART A

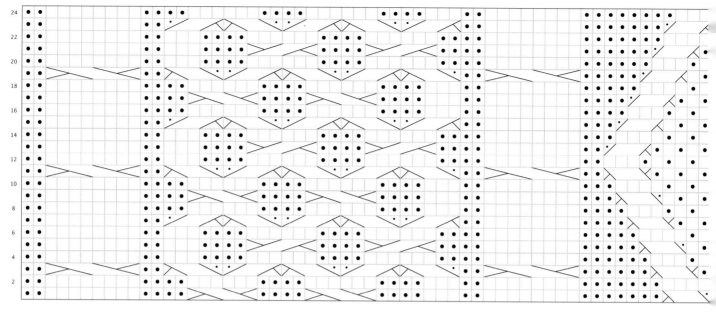

KEY

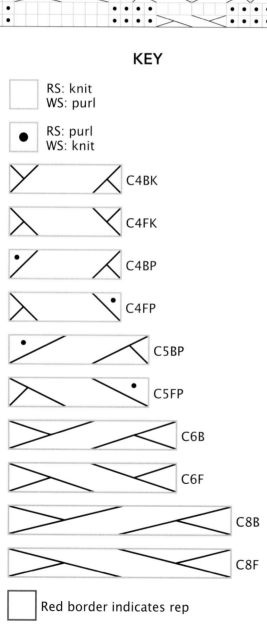

	RS: knit WS: purl
●	RS: purl WS: knit

C4BK

C4FK

C4BP

C4FP

C5BP

C5FP

C6B

C6F

C8B

C8F

	Red border indicates rep

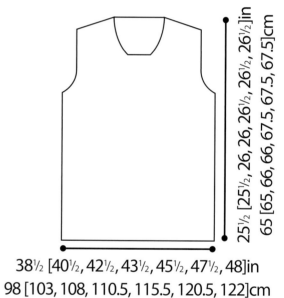

25½ [25½, 26, 26, 26½, 26½, 26½]in
65 [65, 66, 66, 67.5, 67.5, 67.5]cm

38½ [40½, 42½, 43½, 45½, 47½, 48]in
98 [103, 108, 110.5, 115.5, 120.5, 122]cm

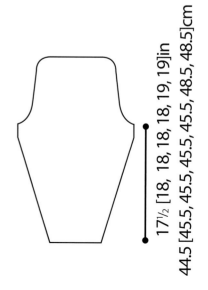

17½ [18, 18, 18, 18, 19, 19]in
44.5 [45.5, 45.5, 45.5, 45.5, 48.5, 48.5]cm

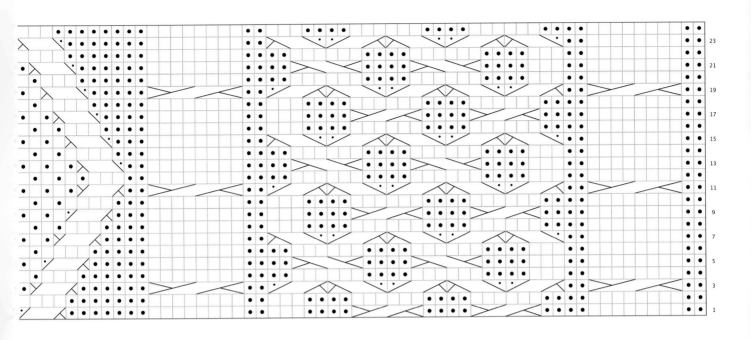

DIAMOND CABLED PULLOVER CHART B

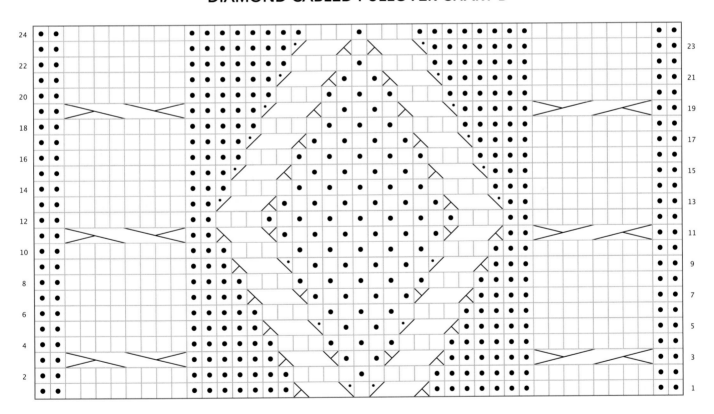

CABLED BERET

Skill Level ★

MEASUREMENTS AND YARN

Size	One size only	
Diameter	12 30.5	in cm
Rhichard Devrieze Yarns, Peppino (100% merino wool) in Visions of Paradise	2	$2^{3/10}$oz/65g 225yds/206m skeins

OTHER MATERIALS

• 1 pair US 3 (3.25mm) knitting needles OR SIZE TO OBTAIN GAUGE

• 1 pair of US 6 (4mm) knitting needles OR SIZE TO OBTAIN GAUGE

• Cable needle

Gauge: 22 sts and 28 rows = 4in/10cm in St st with larger needles.

TAKE TIME TO CHECK GAUGE.

SPECIAL ABBREVIATIONS

s2kpo: Slip 2tog as if to knit, K1, pass slip sts over.

s2ppo: Slip 2tog as if to purl, P1, pass slip sts over.

C6F: Slip next 3 sts onto a cable needle and hold at front, K3, K3 from cable needle.

C6B: Slip next 3 sts onto a cable needle and hold at back, K3, K3 from cable needle.

BERET

Using smaller needles, cast on 115 sts.

Row 1: K1, *P1, K1, rep from * to end.

Row 2: P1, *K1, P1, rep from * to end.

Rep the last 2 rows 4 times more, then Row 1 again.

Next Row: P1, *Kfb, rib 1, Kfb, rib 2, rep from * to last 4 sts, [Kfb, P1] twice—161 sts.

Change to larger needles.

Row 1 (RS): K4, P2, K9, P2, *K7, P2, K9, P2, rep from * to last 4 sts, K4.

Row 2: P4, K2, P9, K2, *P7, K2, P9, K2, rep from * to last 4 sts, P4.

Row 3: K1, *m1, K3, P2, K3, C6F, P2, K3, m1, K1, rep from * to end—177 sts.

Rows 4 and 6: P5, K2, *P9, K2, rep from * to last 5 sts, P5.

Row 5: K5, P2, *K9, P2, rep from * to last 5 sts, K5.

Row 7: K1, *m1, K4, P2, C6B, K3, P2, K4, m1, K1, rep from * to end—193 sts.

Rows 8 and 10: P6, K2, P9, K2, *P11, K2, P9, K2, rep from * to last 6 sts, P6.

Row 9: K6, P2, K9, P2, *K11, P2, K9, P2, rep from * to last 6 sts, K6.

Row 11: K1, *m1, K5, P2, K3, C6F, P2, K5, m1, K1, rep from * to end—209 sts.

Rows 12 and 14: P7, K2, P9, K2, *P13, K2, P9, K2, rep from * to last 7 sts, P7.

Row 13: K7, P2, K9, P2, *K13, P2, K9, P2, rep from * to last 7 sts, K7.

Row 15: K1, *m1, K6, P2, C6B, K3, P2, K6, m1, K1, rep from * to end—225 sts.

Rows 16 and 18: P8, K2, P9, K2, *P15, K2, P9, K2, rep from * to last 8 sts, P8.

Row 17: K8, P2, K9, P2, *K15, P2, K9, P2, rep from * to last 8 sts, K8.

Row 19: K1, *m1, K7, P2, K3, C6F, P2, K7, m1, K1, rep from * to end—241 sts.

Rows 20 and 22: [P9, K2] twice, *P17, K2, P9, K2, rep from * to last 9 sts, P9.

Row 21: [K9, P2] twice, *K17, P2, K9, P2, rep from * to last 9 sts, K9.

Row 23: K1, *K2tog, K6, P2, C6B, K3, P2, K6, skpo, K1, rep from * to end—225 sts.

Rows 24–26: Rep Rows 16–18.

Row 27: K1, *K2tog, K5, P2, K3, C6F, P2, K5, skpo, K1, rep from * to end—209 sts.

Rows 28–30: Rep Rows 12–14.

Row 31: K1, *K2tog, K4, P2, C6B, K3, P2, K4, skpo, K1, rep from * to end—193 sts.

Rows 32–34: Rep Rows 8–10.

Row 35: K1, *K2tog, K3, P2, K3, C6F, P2, K3, skpo, K1, rep from * to end—177 sts.

Rows 36–38: Rep Rows 4–6.

Row 39: K1, *K2tog, K2, P2, C6B, K3, P2, K2, skpo, K1, rep from * to end—161 sts.

Row 40: Rep Row 2.

Rows 41 and 42: Rep Rows 1 and 2.

Row 43: K1, *K2tog, K1, P2, K3, C6F, P2, K1, skpo, K1, rep from * to end—145 sts.

Rows 44 and 46: P3, K2, P9, K2, *P5, K2, P9, K2, rep from * to last 3 sts, P3.

Row 45: K3, P2, K9, P2, *K5, P2, K9, P2, rep from * to last 3 sts, K3.

Row 47: K1, *K2tog, P2, C6B, K3, P2, skpo, K1, rep from * to end—129 sts.

Rows 48 and 50: P2, K2, P9, K2, *P3, K2, P9, K2, rep from * to last 2 sts, P2.

Row 49: K2, P2, K9, P2, *K3, P2, K9, P2, rep from * to last 2 sts, K2.

Row 51: K2tog, P2, K3, C6F, P2, *s2kpo, P2, K3, C6F, P2, rep from * to last 2 sts, skpo—113 sts.

Row 52: P1, *K2, P9, K2, P1, rep from * to end.

Row 53: K1, *P2tog, K9, P2tog, K1, rep from * to end—97 sts.

Row 54: P1, *K1, P9, K1, P1, rep from * to end.

Row 55: K1, *P1, slip next 2 sts onto a cable needle and hold at back of work, K2, K2tog, then K2 from cable needle, K2tog, K1, P1, K1, rep from * to end—81 sts.

Row 56: P1, *K1, P1, [P2tog, P1] twice, K1, P1, rep from * to end—65 sts.

Row 57: K1, *P1, K2tog, K1, K2tog, P1, K1, rep from * to end—49 sts.

Row 58: P1, *K1, s2ppo, K1, P1, rep from * to end—33 sts.

Row 59: K1, *s2kpo, K1, rep from * to end—17 sts.

Row 60: P1, [P2tog] to end—9 sts.

Break off yarn leaving an end, thread through rem sts, pull up tightly and fasten off securely.

FINISHING

Join row ends together. This seam will run at center back of beret.

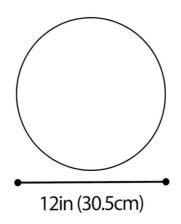

12in (30.5cm)

TUNIC SWEATER

Skill Level ★★★

MEASUREMENTS AND YARN

To fit bust	34 86.5	36 91.5	38 96.5	40 101.5	42 106.5	in cm
Actual size	38 96.5	40½ 103	43½ 110.5	44½ 113	47 119.5	in cm
Full Length (approximately)	27½ 70	28½ 72.5	29½ 75	31 78.5	31½ 80	in cm
Sleeve Length (adjustable)	16½ 42	17½ 44.5	17½ 44.5	18 45.5	18 45.5	in cm
Blue Sky Fibers Extra (55% alpaca/45% merino wool) in #3514 Marsh	10	11	12	12	14	1¾oz/150g 218yds/199m hanks

OTHER MATERIALS

- 1 pair US 6 (4mm) knitting needles OR SIZE TO OBTAIN GAUGE

- 1 pair US 8 (5mm) knitting needles OR SIZE TO OBTAIN GAUGE

- Stitch holders

- Cable needle

Gauge: 29 sts and 27 rows = 4in/10cm over cable patt using US 8 (5mm) needles.

TAKE TIME TO CHECK GAUGE.

SPECIAL ABBREVIATIONS

C4B: Slip next 2 sts onto a cable needle and hold at back, K2, then K2 from cable needle.

C4F: Slip next 2 sts onto a cable needle and hold at front, K2, then K2 from cable needle.

C4BP: Slip next st onto a cable needle and hold at back, K3, then P1 from cable needle.

C4FP: Slip next 3 sts onto a cable needle and hold at front, P1, then K3 from cable needle.

C6B: Slip next 3 sts onto a cable needle and hold at back, K3, then K3 from cable needle.

C6F: Slip next 3 sts onto a cable needle and hold at front, K3, then K3 from cable needle.

C6BP: Slip next 3 sts onto a cable needle and hold at back, K3, then P3 from cable needle.

C6FP: Slip next 3 sts onto a cable needle and hold at front, P3, then K3 from cable needle.

SWEATER

BACK

Using larger needles cast on 140 (148, 160, 164, 172) sts.

Row 1 (RS): P3 (1, 1, 3, 1), [K4, P2] 3 (4, 5, 5, 6) times, work Row 1 of chart A over next 98 sts, [P2, K4] 3 (4, 5, 5, 6) times, P3 (1, 1, 3, 1).

Row 2: K3 (1, 1, 3, 1), [P4, K2] 3 (4, 5, 5, 6) times, work Row 2 of chart A over next 98 sts, [K2, P4] 3 (4, 5, 5, 6) times, K3 (1, 1, 3, 1).

Row 3: P3 (1, 1, 3, 1), [C4B, P2] 3 (4, 5, 5, 6) times, work Row 3 of chart A over next 98 sts, [P2, C4F] 3 (4, 5, 5, 6) times, P3 (1, 1, 3, 1).

Row 4: K3 (1, 1, 3, 1), [P4, K2] 3 (4, 5, 5, 6) times, work Row 4 of chart A over next 98 sts, [K2, P4] 3 (4, 5, 5, 6) times, K3 (1, 1, 3, 1).

These last 4 rows set position of chart A with cables at either side.

Work even as set working appropriate rows of chart until back measures 18 (18, 19, 19¾, 19¾)in/45.5 (45.5, 48.5, 50, 50)cm, ending with RS facing for next row.

Shape raglans

Keeping patt correct, bind off 4 sts at beg of next 2 rows—132 (140, 152, 156, 164) sts.

Row 3: K2, skpo, work in patt to last 4 sts, K2tog, K2.

Row 4: P3, work in patt to last 3 sts, P3.

Rep Rows 3 and 4 until 86 (86, 100, 100, 108) sts rem, ending with RS facing for next row.

Next Row: K2, skpo, work in patt to last 4 sts, K2tog, K2.

Next Row: P2, P2tog, work in patt to last 4 sts, P2tog tbl, P2.

Rep the last 2 rows until 50 (54, 56, 56, 56) sts rem, ending with RS facing for next row.

Slip rem 50 (54, 56, 56, 56) sts onto a st holder.

FRONT

Work as given for back until 86 (90, 96, 96, 100) sts rem in raglan shaping, ending with RS facing for next row.

Shape neck

Next row (RS): K2, skpo, work in patt over 25 (26, 29, 28, 30) sts, slip rem sts onto a st holder. Turn.

Cont on these 28 (29, 32, 31, 33) sts for first side of neck.

2nd size only

Next row (WS): Patt2tog, work in patt to last 3 sts, P3.

Next row: K2, skpo, work in patt to last 2 sts, patt2tog.

Rep the last 2 rows once more, ending with WS facing for next row—23 sts.

All sizes

Next row (WS): Patt2tog, work in patt to last 4 sts, P2tog tbl, P2.

Next row: K2, skpo, work in patt to last 2 sts, patt2tog.

Rep the last 2 rows 3 (2, 4, 4, 4) times more—12 (11, 12, 11, 13) sts.

1st and 3rd sizes only

Next row (WS): Patt2tog, work in patt to last 4 sts, P2tog tbl, P2—10 sts.

All sizes

Dec 1 st as before at raglan edge only on every row until 4 sts rem.

Next row (RS): K2, skpo—3 sts.

Next row: P2tog tbl, P1—2 sts.

Next row: Skpo and fasten off.

With RS facing, leave center 28 (30, 30, 32, 32) sts on holder, place rem sts on needle, rejoin yarn and work in patt to last 4 sts, K2tog, K2—28 (29, 32, 31, 33) sts.

Work to match first side, reversing all shapings.

SLEEVES (Make 2)

Using larger needles cast on 74 (86, 86, 86, 98) sts.

Row 1 (RS): K2, [P2, K4] 2 (3, 3, 3, 4) times, P2, work Row 1 of chart B over next 42 sts, P2, [K4, P2] 2 (3, 3, 3, 4) times, K2.

Row 2: P2, [K2, P4] 2 (3, 3, 3, 4) times, K2, work Row 2 of chart B over next 42 sts, K2, [P4, K2] 2 (3, 3, 3, 4) times, P2.

Row 3: K2, [P2, C4B] 2 (3, 3, 3, 4) times, P2, work Row 3 of chart B over next 42 sts, P2, [C4F, P2] 2 (3, 3, 3, 4) times, K2.

Row 4: P2, [K2, P4] 2 (3, 3, 3, 4) times, K2, work Row 4 of chart B over next 42 sts, K2, [P4, K2] 2 (3, 3, 3, 4) times, P2.

These last 4 rows set position of chart B with cables at either side.

Work even as set, working appropriate rows of chart, AT THE SAME TIME inc 1 st at each end of next and every foll 6th (4th, 4th, 4th, 4th) row until there are 100 (122, 122, 124, 134) sts, working inc sts into patt.

Work even until sleeve measures 16½ (17½, 17½, 18, 18) in/42 (44.5, 44.5, 45.5, 45.5)cm, ending with RS facing for next row.

Shape raglans

Keeping patt correct, bind off 4 sts at beg of next 2 rows—92 (114, 114, 116, 126) sts.

Row 3: K2, skpo, work in patt to last 4 sts, K2tog, K2.

Row 4: P3, work in patt to last 3 sts, P3.

Rep Rows 3 and 4 until 46 (78, 70, 66, 78) sts rem, ending with RS facing for next row.

Next row: K2, skpo, patt to last 4 sts, K2tog, K2.

Next row: P2, P2tog, patt to last 4 sts, P2tog tbl, P2.

Rep the last 2 rows until 10 sts rem, ending with RS facing for next row.

Slip these rem 10 sts onto a st holder.

NECKBAND

Join raglans, leaving left back raglan open.

With RS facing and using smaller needles, K10 from left sleeve, pick up and K12 (12, 14, 16, 16) sts down left side of neck, K28 (30, 30, 32, 32) sts from center front of neck, pick up and K12 (12, 14, 16, 16) sts up right side of neck, K10 across right sleeve, then K across 50 (54, 56, 56, 56) sts left on a st holder for back of neck—122 (128, 134, 140, 140) sts.

Row 1 (WS): K2, [P4, K2] to end.

Row 2: P2, [C4F, P2] to end.

Row 3: Rep Row 1.

Row 4: P2, [K4, P2] to end.

The last 4 rows form cabled ribbing.

Work 13 rows more in ribbing, ending with RS facing for next row.

Bind off loosely in patt.

FINISHING

Join left back raglan and neckband.

Join side and sleeve seams.

TUNIC SWEATER CHART A

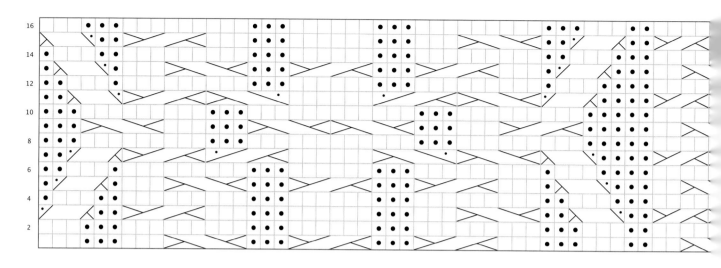

KEY

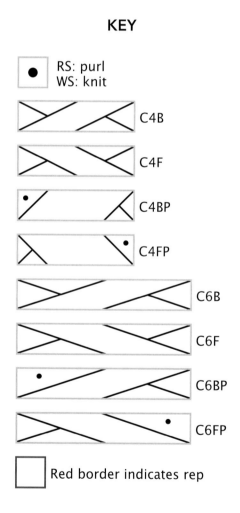

- • RS: purl
  WS: knit
- C4B
- C4F
- C4BP
- C4FP
- C6B
- C6F
- C6BP
- C6FP
- ☐ Red border indicates rep

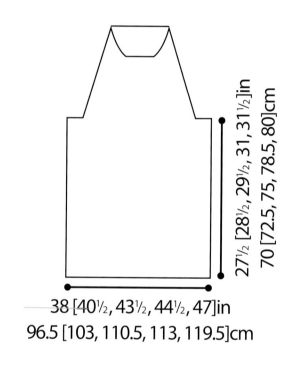

27½ [28½, 29½, 31, 31½]in
70 [72.5, 75, 78.5, 80]cm

38 [40½, 43½, 44½, 47]in
96.5 [103, 110.5, 113, 119.5]cm

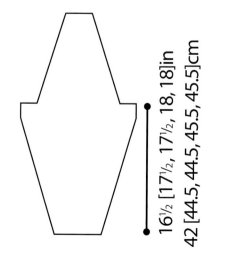

16½ [17½, 17½, 18, 18]in
42 [44.5, 44.5, 45.5, 45.5]cm

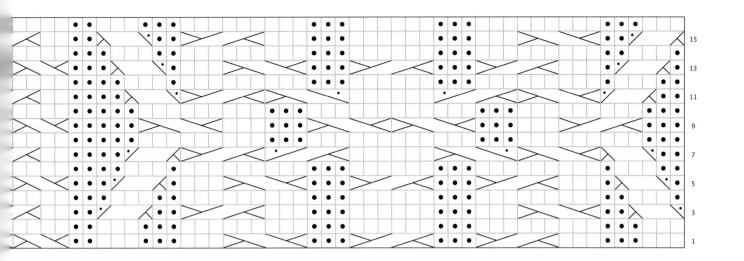

TUNIC SWEATER CHART B

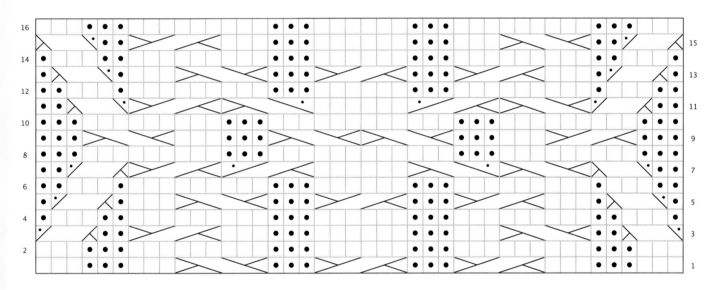

GRANDFATHER CARDIGAN

Skill Level ★★

MEASUREMENTS AND YARN

To fit bust	32–34 81.5–86.5	36–38 91.5–97	40–42 101.5–106.5	44–46 112–117	in cm
Actual size	41½ 105.5	45¾ 116	50 127	54¼ 138	in cm
Full Length (approximately)	25 63.5	25½ 65	26 66	26½ 67.5	in cm
Sleeve Length (adjustable)	18 45.5	18 45.5	18 45.5	18 45.5	in cm
MillaMia Naturally Soft Aran (100% merino wool) in #233 Damson	14	16	18	20	1¾oz/50g 87yds/80m balls

OTHER MATERIALS

• 1 pair US 5 (3.75mm) knitting needles OR SIZE TO OBTAIN GAUGE

• 1 pair US 7 (4.5mm) knitting needles OR SIZE TO OBTAIN GAUGE

• 1 US 5 (3.75mm) 32in/81.5cm circular needle OR SIZE TO OBTAIN GAUGE

• Cable needle

• Stitch holders

• 5 buttons

Gauge: 19 sts and 26 rows = 4in/10cm over St st using US 7 (4.5mm) needles.

TAKE TIME TO CHECK GAUGE.

SPECIAL ABBREVIATIONS

C3BP: Slip next st onto a cable needle and hold at back, K2, then P1 from cable needle.

C3FP: Slip next 2 sts onto a cable needle and hold at front, P1, then K2 from cable needle.

C4B: Slip next 2 sts onto a cable needle and hold at back, K2, then K2 from cable needle.

C4F: Slip next 2 sts onto a cable needle and hold at front, K2, then K2 from cable needle.

CARDIGAN

BACK

Using smaller needles cast on 114 (126, 138, 150) sts.

Row 1 (RS): P0 (2, 0, 2), [K2, P2] 3 (3, 4, 4) times, *[K2, P3] twice, K2, P2, K2, [P3, K2] twice, [P2, K2] 1 (2, 3, 4) times, P2, rep from * once more, [K2, P3] twice, K2, P2, K2, [P3, K2] twice, [P2, K2] 3 (3, 4, 4) times, P0 (2, 0, 2).

Row 2: K0 (2, 0, 2), [P2, K2] 3 (3, 4, 4) times, *[P2, K3] twice, P2, K2, P2, [K3, P2] twice, [K2, P2] 1 (2, 3, 4) times, K2, rep from * once more, [P2, K3] twice, P2, K2, P2, [K3, P2] twice, [K2, P2] 3 (3, 4, 4) times, K0 (2, 0, 2).

The last 2 rows set ribbing.

Work 14 more rows in ribbing as set, ending with RS facing for next row.

Change to larger needles.

Row 1 (RS): K10 (12, 14, 16), work Row 1 of chart over next 30 sts, K34 (42, 50, 58), work Row 1 of chart over next 30 sts, K10 (12, 14, 16).

Row 2: P10 (12, 14, 16), work Row 2 of chart over next 30 sts, P34 (42, 50, 58), work Row 2 of chart over next 30 sts, P10 (12, 14, 16).

The last 2 rows set chart and St st on either side and in between.

Work even as set, working appropriate rows of chart until back measures 15¾in/40cm, ending with RS facing for next row. Place a marker at each end of last row to mark start of armholes.

Cont in patt until back measures 25 (25½, 26, 26½)in/63.5 (65, 66, 67.5)cm, ending with RS facing for next row.

Shape shoulders

Keeping patt correct, bind off 9 (10, 10, 11) st at beg of next 4 rows, then 8 (9, 10, 11) sts at beg of next 6 rows—30 (32, 38, 40) sts.

Place rem 30 (32, 38, 40) sts on a st holder.

POCKET LININGS (Make 2)

Using larger needles, cast on 30 sts and work 30 rows in St st, beg with a K row, ending with RS facing for next row. Leave these st on a st holder.

LEFT FRONT

Using smaller needles cast on 54 (60, 66, 72) sts.

Row 1 (RS): P0 (2, 0, 2), [K2, P2] 3 (3, 4, 4) times, [K2, P3] twice, K2, P2, K2, [P3, K2] twice, [P2, K2] 4 (5, 6, 7) times.

Row 2: [P2, K2] 4 (5, 6, 7) times, [P2, K3] twice, P2, K2, P2, [K3, P2] twice, [K2, P2] 3 (3, 4, 4) times, K0 (2, 0, 2).

The last 2 rows form ribbing.

Work 14 more rows in ribbing as set, ending with RS facing for next row.

Change to larger needles.

Row 1 (RS): K10 (12, 14, 16), work Row 1 of chart over next 30 sts, K14 (18, 22, 26).

Row 2: P14 (18, 22, 26), work Row 2 of chart over next 30 sts, P10 (12, 14, 16).

The last 2 rows set chart and St st either side.

Work even as set for 30 more rows, working appropriate rows of chart.

Place pocket

Next Row (RS): K10 (12, 14, 16), slip next 30 sts onto a st holder, with RS facing, work in patt across 30 sts of one pocket lining, K14 (18, 22, 26).

Work even in patt until left front measures 13¾in/35cm, ending with RS facing for next row.

Shape neck

Next Row (RS): Work in patt to last 4 sts, K2tog, K2.

Next 3 Rows: Work even in patt.

Cont in patt, dec 1 st at neck edge as before on next and every foll 4th row until 48 (53, 57, 62) sts rem, then on every foll 6th row until 42 (47, 50, 55) sts rem, placing a marker at armhole edge to correspond with marker on back.

Work even in patt until left front matches back to start of shoulder shaping, ending with RS facing for next row.

Shape shoulder

Keeping patt correct, bind off 9 (10, 10, 11) sts at beg of next row and foll RS row, then 8 (9, 10, 11) sts at beg of foll 3 RS rows.

RIGHT FRONT

Using smaller needles cast on 54 (60, 66, 72) sts.

Row 1 (RS): [K2, P2] 4 (5, 6, 7) times, [K2, P3] twice, K2, P2, K2, [P3, K2] twice, [P2, K2] 3 (3, 4, 4) times, P0 (2, 0, 2).

Row 2: K0 (2, 0, 2), [P2, K2] 3 (3, 4, 4) times, [P2, K3] twice, P2, K2, P2, [K3, P2] twice, [K2, P2] 4 (5, 6: 7) times.

The last 2 rows form ribbing.

Work 14 more rows in ribbing as set, ending with RS facing for next row.

Change to larger needles.

Row 1 (RS): K14 (18, 22, 26), work Row 1 of chart over next 30 sts, K10 (12, 14, 16).

Row 2: P10 (12, 14, 16), work Row 2 of chart over next 30 sts, P14 (18, 22, 26).

The last 2 rows set chart and St st either side.

Work even as set for 30 more rows, working appropriate rows of chart.

Place pocket

Next Row (RS): K14 (18, 22, 26), slip next 30 sts onto a st holder, with RS facing, work in patt across 30 sts of rem pocket lining, K10 (12, 14, 16).

Work even in patt until left front measures 13¾in/35cm, ending with RS facing for next row.

Shape neck

Next Row: K2, skpo, work in patt to end.

Next 3 Rows: Work even in patt.

Cont in patt, dec 1 st at neck edge as before on next and every foll 4th row until 48 (53, 57, 62) sts rem, then on every foll 6th row until 42 (47, 50, 55) sts rem, placing a marker at armhole edge to correspond with marker on back.

Work even in patt until right front matches back to start of shoulder shaping, ending with WS facing for next row.

Shape shoulder

Keeping patt correct, bind off 9 (10, 10, 11) sts at beg of next and foll WS row, then 8 (9, 10, 11) sts at beg of foll 3 WS rows.

SLEEVES (Make 2)

Using smaller needles cast on 54 (58, 62, 66) sts.

Row 1 (RS): P2 (0, 2, 0), [K2, P2] 3 (4, 4, 5) times, [K2, P3] twice, K2, P2, K2, [P3, K2] twice, [P2, K2] 3 (4, 4, 5) times, P2 (0, 2, 0).

Row 2: K2 (0, 2, 0), [P2, K2] 3 (4, 4, 5) times, [P2, K3] twice, P2, K2, P2, [K3, P2] twice, [K2, P2] 3 (4, 4, 5) times, K2 (0, 2, 0).

The last 2 rows form ribbing.

Work 14 more rows in ribbing as set, ending with RS facing for next row.

Change to larger needles.

Row 1 (RS): K12 (14, 16, 18), work Row 1 of chart over next 30 sts, K12 (14, 16, 18).

Row 2: P12 (14, 16, 18), work Row 2 of chart over next 30 sts, P12 (14, 16, 18).

The last 2 rows set chart and St st either side.

Cont as set working appropriate rows of chart and AT THE SAME TIME inc 1 st at each end of next and every 6th row until there are 80 (86, 90, 94) sts, working all inc sts in St st.

Work even in patt until sleeve measures 18in (45.5cm), ending with RS facing for next row.

Bind off loosely in patt.

RIGHT FRONT BORDER

Join shoulder seams.

With RS facing and circular needle, pick up and K76 sts up right front to start of neck shaping, pick up and K63 (66, 67, 70) sts along right front neck slope to shoulder, then K15 (16, 19, 20) sts from back neck, leaving rem back neck sts on a st holder—154 (158, 162, 166) sts.

Row 1 (WS): P2, *K2, P2, rep from * to end.

Row 2: K2, *P2, K2, rep from * to end.

Row 3: Rep Row 1.

Row 4: Rib 3, bind off 3 sts, [rib 13 including st on needle, bind off 3 sts] 4 times, work in ribbing to end.

Row 5: Rep Row 1 and AT THE SAME TIME cast on 3 sts over the bound-off sts in previous row.

Row 6: Rep Row 2.

Row 7: Rep Row 1.

Row 8: Rep Row 2.

Bind off in ribbing.

LEFT FRONT BORDER

With RS facing and circular needle, K15 (16, 19, 20) sts from back neck holder, pick up and K63 (66, 67, 70) sts down left front neck slope, then pick up and K76 sts down left front—154 (158, 162, 166) sts.

Row 1 (WS): P2, *K2, P2, rep from * to end.

Row 2: K2, *P2, K2, rep from * to end.

Rep the last 2 rows 3 times more.

Bind off in ribbing.

POCKET TOPS

With RS facing and using smaller needles rejoin yarn and work across the 30 sts of pocket top as follows:

Row 1 (WS): P2, *K2, P2, rep from * to end.

Row 2: K2, *P2, K2, rep from * to end.

Rep the last 2 rows twice more.

Bind off in ribbing.

FINISHING

Join neck border neatly together at center back of neck. Pin bound-off edges of sleeves between markers on back and front, sew in position, then join side and sleeve seams. Sew pocket linings neatly to WS. Sew pocket top ribbing row ends neatly in place. Sew on buttons to correspond with buttonholes.

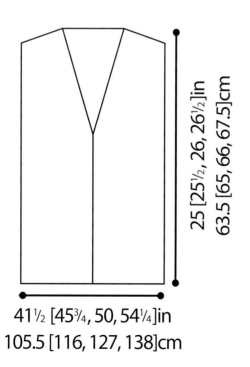

25 [25½, 26, 26½]in
63.5 [65, 66, 67.5]cm

41½ [45¾, 50, 54¼]in
105.5 [116, 127, 138]cm

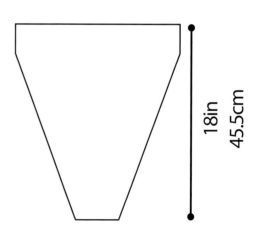

18in
45.5cm

KEY

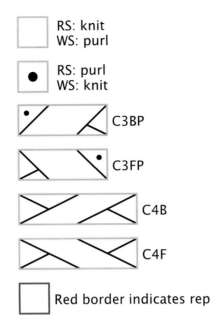

☐ RS: knit
WS: purl

⬛ RS: purl
WS: knit

◨ C3BP

◨ C3FP

▭ C4B

▭ C4F

☐ Red border indicates rep

GRANDFATHER CARDIGAN CHART

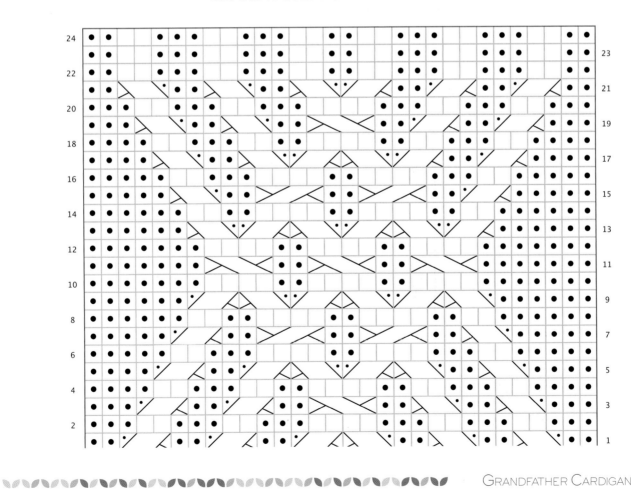

TWO-COLOR CARDIGAN

Skill Level ★★

MEASUREMENTS AND YARN

To fit bust	32–34 81.5–86.5	36–38 91.5–96.5	40–42 101.5–106.5	44–46 112–117	48–50 122–127	52–54 132–137	in cm
Actual size	36 91.5	40 101.5	44 112	48 122	52 132	56 142	in cm
Full Length (approximately)	26 66	26¾ 68	28¼ 72	30 76	31½ 80	33 84	in cm
Sleeve Length (adjustable)	18 45.5	18 45.5	18½ 47	19 48.5	19 48.5	19½ 49.5	in cm
Plymouth Yarn® Galway Highland Heather (100% worsted wool) in #754 Turtle Heather (A)	7	8	9	10	11	12	3½oz/100g 218yds/200m balls
Plymouth Yarn® Galway Highland Heather (100% worsted wool) in #765 Rustic (B)	1	1	1	1	1	1	3.5oz/100g 218yds/200m balls

OTHER MATERIALS

• 1 pair US 6 (4mm) knitting needles OR SIZE TO OBTAIN GAUGE

• 1 pair US 8 (5mm) knitting needles OR SIZE TO OBTAIN GAUGE

• Cable needle

• Stitch holders

• 7 (7, 8, 8, 9, 9) buttons

Gauge: 18 sts and 24 rows = 4in/10cm over St st using US 8 (5mm) needles.

TAKE TIME TO CHECK GAUGE.

SPECIAL ABBREVIATIONS

C3BK: Slip next st onto a cable needle and hold at back, K2, then K1 from cable needle.

C3FK: Slip next 2 sts onto a cable needle and hold at front, K1, then K2 from cable needle.

C3BP: Slip next st onto a cable needle and hold at back, K2, then P1 from cable needle.

C3FP: Slip next 2 sts onto a cable needle and hold at front, P1, then K2 from cable needle.

C4B: Slip next 2 sts onto a cable needle and hold at back, K2, then K2 from cable needle.

C4F: Slip next 2 sts onto a cable needle and hold at front, K2, then K2 from cable needle.

CARDIGAN

BACK

Using smaller needles and yarn B, cast on 90 (98, 106, 118, 126, 134) sts.

Row 1 (RS): K2, *P2, K2, rep from * to end.

Row 2: P2, *K2, P2, rep from * to end.

The last 2 rows form ribbing.

Change to yarn A and work 13 more rows in ribbing as set, ending with WS facing for next row.

Next row (WS): Rib 3 (7, 11, 17, 21, 25), m1, [rib 2, m1] 19 times, [rib 4, m1] twice, [rib 2, m1] 19 times, rib 3 (7, 11, 17, 21, 25)—131 (139, 147, 159, 167, 175) sts.

Change to larger needles.

Row 1 (RS): K3 (7, 11, 17, 21, 25), work Row 1 of chart A over next 125 sts, K3 (7, 11, 17, 21, 25).

Row 2: P3 (7, 11, 17, 21, 25), work Row 2 of chart A over next 125 sts, P3 (7, 11, 17, 21, 25).

The last 2 rows position chart A with St st either side.

Work even in patt as set, working appropriate row of chart until back measures 17½ (17½, 18, 19, 19¾, 21¼) in/44.5 (44.5, 45.5, 48.5, 50, 54)cm, ending with RS facing for next row.

Shape raglan

Keeping patt correct, bind off 6 sts at beg of next 2 rows—119 (127, 135, 147, 155, 163) sts.

Next row (RS): K2, skpo, work in patt to last 4 sts, K2tog, K2.

Next row: P2, P2tog, work in patt to last 4 sts, P2tog tbl, P2.

The last 2 rows set raglan shaping.

Rep last 2 rows until 39 (47, 47, 51, 51, 51) sts rem.

Work 3 (7, 7, 7, 7, 3) rows more, dec 1 st at each end of RS rows only, ending with WS facing for next row—35 (39, 39, 43, 43, 47) sts.

Next row (WS): P4 (3, 3, 2, 2, 4), [patt2tog, P1] 9 (11, 11, 13, 13, 13) times, P4 (3, 3, 2, 2, 4)—26 (28, 28, 30, 30, 34) sts.

Leave these rem 26 (28, 28, 30, 30, 34) sts on a st holder.

LEFT FRONT

Using smaller needles and yarn B, cast on 43 (47, 51, 59, 63, 67) sts.

Row 1 (RS): K2, *P2, K2, rep from * to last st, P1.

Row 2: K1, P2, *K2, P2, rep from * to end.

The last 2 rows form ribbing.

Change to yarn A and work 13 more rows in ribbing as set, ending with WS facing for next row.

Next row (WS): Rib 2 (2, 2, 4, 4, 4), m1, [rib 2, m1] 19 (19, 19, 17, 17, 17) times, rib 3 (7, 11, 21, 25, 29)—63 (67, 71, 77, 81, 85) sts.

Change to larger needles.

Row 1 (RS): K3 (7, 11, 17, 21, 25), work Row 1 of chart B over next 58 sts, P2.

Row 2: K2, work Row 2 of chart B over next 58 sts, P3 (7, 11, 17, 21, 25).

The last 2 rows position chart B with St st either side.

Work even as set, working appropriate row of chart until left front measures 17½ (17½, 18, 19, 19¾, 21¼)in/44.5 (44.5, 45.5, 48.5, 50, 54)cm, ending with RS facing for next row.

Shape raglan

Keeping patt correct, bind off 6 sts, work in patt to end—57 (61, 65, 71, 75, 79) sts.

Next row (WS): Work even in patt.

Next row: K2, skpo, work in patt to end.

Next row: Work in patt to last 4 sts, P2tog tbl, P2.

The last 2 rows set the raglan shaping.

Rep the last 2 rows until 25 (25, 27, 29, 31, 35) sts rem.

Next row (RS): K2, skpo, work in patt to last 7 sts, [patt-2tog, patt1] twice, patt 1—22 (22, 24, 26, 28, 32) sts.

Shape neck

Keeping patt correct, bind off 6 (8, 8, 8, 8, 10) sts, work in patt to last 4 sts, P2tog tbl, P2—15 (13, 15, 17, 19, 21) sts.

Work 5 (3, 5, 5, 7, 7) rows, dec 1 st at raglan edge as before on every row and AT THE SAME TIME dec 1 st at neck edge on every row—5 (7, 5, 7, 5, 7) sts.

For 1st and 6th sizes only

Work 2 (4) rows, dec 1 st at raglan edge only as before on every row—3 sts.

For 2nd and 4th sizes only

Work 2 rows dec 1 st at raglan edge as before on 2nd row only and AT THE SAME TIME dec 1 st at neck edge on every row—4 sts.

For 2nd, 3rd, 4th and 5th sizes only

Work 2 (4, 2, 4) rows, dec 1 st at raglan edge only as before on 2nd and foll 0 (2nd, 0, 2nd) row—3 sts.

For all 6 sizes

Next row (WS): P3.

Next row: K1, skpo. 2 sts.

Next row: P2tog tbl. Fasten off.

RIGHT FRONT

Using smaller needles and yarn B, cast on 43 (47, 51, 59, 63, 67) sts.

Row 1 (RS): P1, K2, *P2, K2, rep from * to end.

Row 2: P2, *K2, P2, rep from * to last st, K1.

The last 2 rows form rib.

Change to yarn A and work 13 more rows in ribbing as set, ending with WS facing for next row.

Next row (WS): Rib 3 (7, 11, 21, 25, 29), m1, [rib 2, m1] 19 (19, 19, 17, 17, 17) times, rib 2 (2, 2, 4, 4, 4)—63 (67, 71, 77, 81, 85) sts.

Change to larger needles.

Row 1 (RS): P2, work Row 1 chart B over next 58 sts, K3 (7, 11, 17, 21, 25).

Row 2: P3 (7, 11, 17, 21, 25), work Row 2 of chart B over next 58 sts, K2.

The last 2 rows position chart B with St st either side.

Work even as set, working appropriate row of chart until right front measures 17½ (17½, 18, 19, 19¾, 21¼)in/44.5 (44.5, 45.5, 48.5, 50, 54)cm, ending with WS facing for next row.

Shape raglan

Keeping patt correct, bind off 6 sts, work in patt to end—57 (61, 65, 71, 75, 79) sts.

Next row (RS): Work in patt to last 4 sts, K2tog, K2.

Next row: P2, P2tog, work in patt to end.

The last 2 rows set the raglan shaping.

Rep the last 2 rows until 26 (26, 28, 30, 32, 36) sts rem.

Next row (WS): P2, P2tog, work in patt to last 7 sts, [patt-2tog, patt 1] twice, patt 1—23 (23, 25, 27, 29, 33) sts.

Shape neck

Keeping patt correct, bind off 6 (8, 8, 8, 8, 10) sts, work in patt to last 4 sts, K2tog, K2—16 (14, 16, 18, 20, 22) sts.

Next row (WS): P2, P2tog, work in patt to end—15 (13, 15, 17, 19, 21) sts.

Work 5 (3, 5, 5, 7, 7) rows, dec 1 st at neck edge on every row and AT THE SAME TIME dec 1 st at raglan edge as before on every row—5 (7, 5, 7, 5, 7) sts.

For 1st and 6th sizes only

Work 2 (4) rows, dec 1 st at raglan edge only as before on every row—3 sts.

For 2nd and 4th sizes only

Work 2 rows, dec 1 st at raglan edge as before on 2nd row only and AT THE SAME TIME dec 1 st at neck edge on every row—4 sts.

For 2nd, 3rd, 4th and 5th sizes only

Work 2 (4, 2, 4) rows, dec 1 st at raglan edge as before on 2nd and foll 0 (2nd, 0, 2nd) row—3 sts.

For all sizes

Next row (WS): P3.

Next row: K2tog, K1—2 sts.

Next row: P2tog. Fasten off.

SLEEVES (Make 2)

Using smaller needles and yarn B, cast on 50 (54, 54, 58, 62, 62) sts.

Row 1 (RS): K2, *P2, K2, rep from * to end.

Row 2, P2, *K2, P2, rep from * to end.

The last 2 rows form ribbing.

Change to yarn A and work 13 more rows in ribbing as set, ending with WS facing for next row.

Next row (WS): Rib 18 (20, 20, 22, 24, 24), m1, [rib 2, m1] 7 times, rib 18 (20, 20, 22, 24, 24)—58 (62, 62, 66, 70, 70) sts.

Change to larger needles.

Row 1 (RS): K11 (13, 13, 15, 17, 17), work Row 1 of chart C over next 36 sts, K11 (13, 13, 15, 17, 17).

Row 2: P11 (13, 13, 15, 17, 17), work Row 2 of chart C over next 36 sts, P11 (13, 13, 15, 17, 17).

The last 2 rows position chart C with St st either side.

Work in patt as set, working appropriate row of chart, and AT THE SAME TIME inc 1 st at each end of 3rd (3rd, 3rd, next, next, next) and every foll 6th (6th, 6th, 4th, 4th, 4th) row until there are 84 (88, 94, 102, 108, 108) sts, working extra sts in St st.

Work even until sleeve measures 18 (18, 18½, 19, 19, 19½)in/45.5 (45.5, 47, 48.5, 48.5, 49.5)cm, ending with RS facing for next row.

Shape raglan

Keeping patt correct, bind off 6 sts at beg of next 2 rows—72 (76, 82, 90, 96, 96) sts.

Next row (RS): K2, skpo, work in patt to last 4 sts, K2tog, K2.

Next row: P2, P2tog, work in patt to last 4 sts, P2tog tbl, P2.

The last 2 rows set the raglan shaping.

Work 2 (2, 2, 6, 4, 4) rows, dec 1 st at each end as before on every row—64 (68, 74, 74, 84, 84) sts.

Next row (RS): K2, skpo, work in patt to last 4 sts, K2tog, K2.

Next row: P2, work in patt to last 2 sts, P2.

Dec 1 st at each end as before on next row, then every other row 18 (20, 22, 22, 25, 25 times more—24 (24, 26, 26, 30, 30) sts, ending with WS facing for next row.

Next row (WS): P3, patt 0 (0, 1, 1, 1, 1), [patt2tog] 9 (9, 9, 9, 11, 11) times, patt 0 (0, 1, 1, 1, 1), P3. 15 (15, 17, 17, 19, 19) sts.

Leave rem 15 (15, 17, 17, 19, 19) sts on a st holder.

LEFT FRONT BORDER

With RS facing using yarn A and smaller needles, pick up and K126 (134, 142, 146, 150, 158) sts evenly along front edge.

Row 1 (WS), P2, *K2, P2, rep from * to end.

Row 2: K2, *P2, K2, rep from * to end.

The last 2 rows form ribbing.

Work 4 more rows in ribbing as set.

Change to yarn B and work 2 more rows.

Bind off in rib.

RIGHT FRONT BORDER

With RS facing using yarn A and smaller needles, pick up and K126 (134, 142, 146, 150, 158) sts evenly along front edge.

Row 1 (WS): P2, *K2, P2, rep from * to end.

Row 2: K2, *P2, K2, rep from * to end.

Row 3: Rep Row 1.

Row 4: Rib 2 (3, 4, 2, 2, 2), bind off next 2 sts, [rib 18 (18, 17, 18, 16, 17), bind off next 2 sts] 6 (6, 7, 7, 8, 8) times, rib 2 (3, 3, 2, 2, 2).

Row 5: Rib 2 (3, 3, 2, 2, 2), cast on 2 sts, [rib 18 (19, 17, 18, 16, 17), cast on 2 sts] 6 (6, 7, 7, 8, 8) times, rib 2 (3, 4, 2, 2, 2).

Row 6: Rep Row 2.

Change to yarn B.

Row 7: Rep Row 1.

Row 8: Rep Row 2.

Bind off in ribbing.

COLLAR

Join raglan seams.

With RS facing using yarn A and smaller needles, starting halfway across right front border, pick up and K17 (20, 22, 23, 23, 25) sts evenly along right side of neck, 15 (15, 17, 17, 19, 19) sts from right sleeve, 26 (28, 28, 30, 30, 34) sts from back of neck, 15 (15, 17, 17, 19, 19) sts from left sleeve, 17 (20, 22, 23, 23, 25) sts along left side of neck, ending halfway across left front border—90 (98, 106, 110, 114, 122) sts.

Next row: [K2, P2] 2 (3, 4, 3, 2, 3) times, [K2, Pfb] 24 (24, 24, 28, 32, 32) times, K2, [P2, K2] 2 (3, 4, 3, 2, 3) times—114 (122, 130, 138, 146, 154) sts.

Row 1: P2, *K2, P2, rep from * to end.

Row 2: K2, *P2, K2, rep from * to end.

The last 2 rows form ribbing.

Work 23 more rows in ribbing.

Change to yarn B and work 1 more row.

Next row: [P2, K2] 8 (9, 10, 11, 12, 13) times, [Pfb, P1, K2] 12 times, Pfb, P1, [K2, P2] 8 (9, 10, 11, 12, 13) times—127 (135, 143, 151, 159, 167) sts.

Bind off in ribbing.

FINISHING

Join side and sleeve seams.

Sew on buttons to correspond with buttonholes.

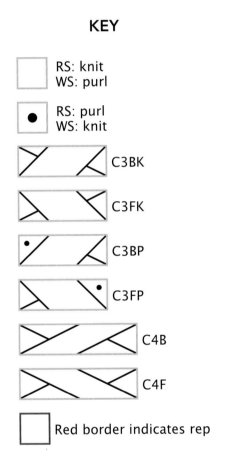

KEY

- ☐ RS: knit / WS: purl
- ▪ RS: purl / WS: knit
- C3BK
- C3FK
- C3BP
- C3FP
- C4B
- C4F
- ☐ Red border indicates rep

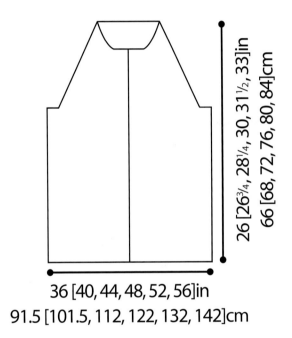

36 [40, 44, 48, 52, 56]in
91.5 [101.5, 112, 122, 132, 142]cm

26 [26¾, 28¼, 30, 31½, 33]in
66 [68, 72, 76, 80, 84]cm

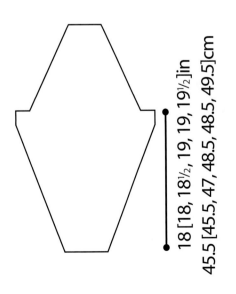

18 [18, 18½, 19, 19, 19½]in
45.5 [45.5, 47, 48.5, 48.5, 49.5]cm

TWO-COLOR CARDIGAN CHART A

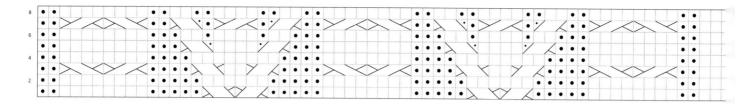

TWO-COLOR CARDIGAN CHART B

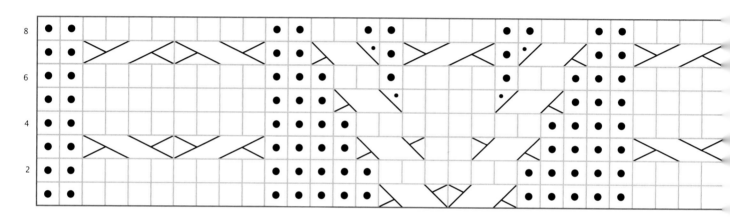

TWO-COLOR CARDIGAN CHART C

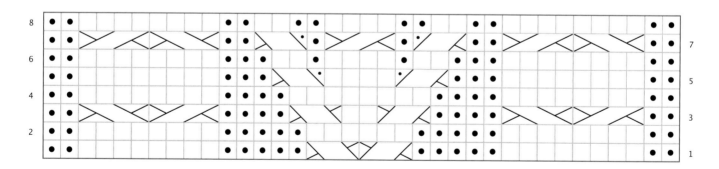

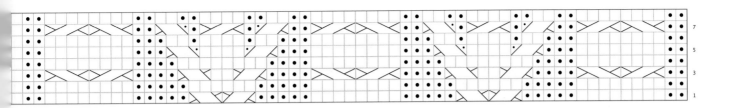

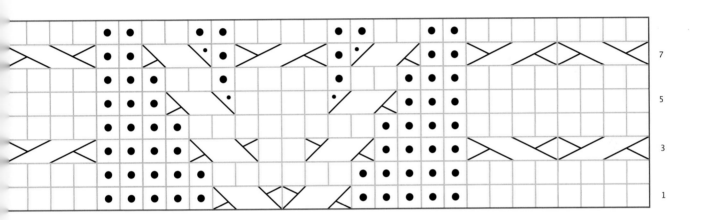

CLASSIC CABLED MITTENS

Skill Level ★

MEASUREMENTS AND YARN

Size	One size only	
Width (approximately)	4 10	in cm
Length (approximately)	8¾ 22	in cm
Knoll Coast DK (55% merino wool, 45% cotton) in #091 Rosehip	2	1¾oz/50g 128yds/117m balls

OTHER MATERIALS

• 1 pair of US 3 [3.25mm] knitting needles OR SIZE TO OBTAIN GAUGE

• 1 pair of US 6 [4mm] knitting needles OR SIZE TO OBTAIN GAUGE

• Cable needle

Gauge: 22 sts and 28 rows = 4in/10cm in St st using US 6 [4mm] needles.

TAKE TIME TO CHECK GAUGE.

SPECIAL ABBREVIATIONS

C4BP: Slip next st onto a cable needle and hold at back, K3, then P1 from cable needle.

C4FP: Slip next 3 sts onto a cable needle and hold at front, P1, then K3 from cable needle.

C5BP: Slip next 2 sts onto a cable needle and hold at back, K3, then P2 from cable needle.

C5FP: Slip next 3 sts onto a cable needle and hold at front, P2, then K3 from cable needle.

C6F: Slip next 3 sts onto a cable needle and hold at front, K3, then K3 from cable needle.

C6B: Slip next 3 sts onto a cable needle and hold at back, K3, then K3 from cable needle.

MITTENS

RIGHT-HAND MITTEN

Using smaller needles cast on 55 sts.

Row 1 [RS]: K1, *P1, K1, rep from * to end.

Row 2: P1, *K1, P1, rep from * to end.

The last 2 rows form ribbing.

Work in ribbing for 5in/12.5cm, ending with WS facing for next row.

Dec row: P2, P2tog, *P3, P2tog, rep from * to last st, P1—44 sts.

Change to larger needles.

Next row (RS): K3, P2, work Row 1 of chart A over next 12 sts, P2, K25.

Next row: P25, K2, work Row 2 of chart A over next 12 sts, K2, P3.

The last 2 rows set chart A and St st either side.

Working appropriate rows of chart A, work 4 more rows in patt, ending with RS facing for next row.

Shape thumb

Row 1 (RS): K3, P2, work Row 7 of chart A over next 12 sts, P2, [K3, m1] twice, K19—46 sts.

Row 2: P27, K2, work Row 8 of chart A over next 12 sts, K2, P3.

Row 3: K3, P2, work Row 9 of chart A over next 12 sts, P2, K3, m1, K5, m1, K19—48 sts.

Row 4: P29, K2, work Row 10 of chart A over next 12 sts, K2, P3.

Row 5: K3, P2, work Row 11 of chart A over next 12 sts, P2, K3, m1, K7, m1, K19—50 sts.

Row 6: P31, K2, work Row 12 of chart A over next 12 sts, K2, P3.

Row 7: K3, P2, work Row 1 of chart A over next 12 sts, P2, K3, m1, K9, m1, K19—52 sts.

Row 8: P33, K2, work Row 2 of chart A over next 12 sts, K2, P3.

Row 9: K3, P2, work Row 3 of chart A over next 12 sts, P2, K3, m1, K11, m1, K19—54 sts.

Row 10: P35, K2, work Row 4 of chart A over next 12 sts, K2, P3.

Row 11: K3, P2, work Row 5 of chart A over next 12 sts,

P2, K3, m1, K13, m1, K19—56 sts.

Row 12: P37, K2, work Row 6 of chart A over next 12 sts, K2, P3.

Divide for thumb

Next row (RS): K3, P2, work Row 7 of chart A over next 12 sts, P2, K18, cast on 1 st, turn.

Next row: P16, cast on 1 st, turn—17 sts.

Working on these 17 sts only, work 12 rows even in St st beg with a K row.

Next row: K1, *K2tog, rep from * to end—9 sts. Break off yarn leaving a long end, thread through rem sts, pull up tightly and fasten off. Join thumb seam.

With RS facing, pick up and K2 sts from base of thumb, K to end—43 sts.

Next row (WS): P24, K2, work Row 8 of chart A over next 12 sts, K2, P to end.

Next row: K3, P2, work Row 9 of chart A over next 12 sts, P2, K to end.

Next row: P24, K2, work Row 10 of chart A over next 12 sts, K2, P to end.

The last 2 rows set chart A and St st either side.

Working appropriate rows of chart A, work 20 more rows in patt, ending with RS facing for next row.

Shape top

Row 1 [RS]: K1, skpo, P2, work Row 7 of chart A over next 12 sts, P2, K2tog, K1, skpo, K16, K2tog, K1—39 sts.

Row 2: P21, K2, work Row 8 of chart A over next 12 sts, K2, P2.

Row 3: K1, skpo, P1, work Row 9 of chart A over next 12 sts, P1, K2tog, K1, skpo, K14, K2tog, K1—35 sts.

Row 4: P1, P2tog, P12, P2tog tbl, P1, P2tog, work Row 10 of chart A over next 12 sts, P2tog tbl, P1—31 sts.

Row 5: K1, skpo, P2, C6B, P2, K2tog, K1, skpo, k10, K2tog, K1—27 sts.

Row 6: P1, P2tog, P8, P2tog tbl, K1, P2tog, K1, P6, K1, P2tog tbl, P1—23 sts.

Bind off in patt.

LEFT-HAND MITTEN

Using smaller needles cast on 55 sts.

Row 1 [RS]: K1, *P1, K1, rep from * to end.

Row 2: P1, *K1, P1, rep from * to end.

The last 2 rows form ribbing.

Work in ribbing for 5in/12.5cm, ending with WS facing for next row.

Dec row: P2, P2tog, *P3, P2tog, rep from * to last st, P1—44 sts.

Change to larger needles.

Next row (RS): K25, P2, work Row 1 of chart B over next 12 sts, P2, K3.

Next row: P3, K2, work Row 2 of chart B over next 12 sts, K2, P25.

The last 2 rows set chart B and St st either side.

Working appropriate rows of chart B, work 4 more rows in patt, ending with RS facing for next row.

Shape thumb

Row 1 (RS): K19, [m1, K3] twice, P2, work Row 7 of chart B over next 12 sts, P2, K3—46 sts.

Row 2: P3, K2, work Row 8 of chart B over next 12 sts, K2, P27.

Row 3: K19, m1, K5, m1, K3, P2, work Row 9 of chart B over next 12 sts, P2, K3,—48 sts.

Row 4: P3, K2, work Row 10 of chart A over next 12 sts, K2, P29.

Row 5: K19, m1, K7, m1, K3, P2, work Row 11 of chart B over next 12 sts, P2, K3—50 sts.

Row 6: P3, K2, work Row 12 of chart B over next 12 sts, K2, P31.

Row 7: K19, m1, K9, m1, K3, P2, work Row 1 of chart B over next 12 sts, P2, K3,—52 sts.

Row 8: P3, K2, work Row 2 of chart B over next 12 sts, K2, P33.

Row 9: K19, m1, K11, m1, K3, P2, work Row 3 of chart B over next 12 sts, P2, K3—54 sts.

Row 10: P3, K2, work Row 4 of chart B over next 12 sts, K2, P35.

Row 11: K19, m1, K13, m1, K3, P2, work Row 5 of chart B over next 12 sts, P2, K3—56 sts.

Row 12: P3, K2, work Row 6 of chart B over next 12 sts, K2, P37.

Divide for thumb

Next row (RS): K34, cast on 1 st, turn.

Next row: P16, cast on 1 st, turn—17 sts.

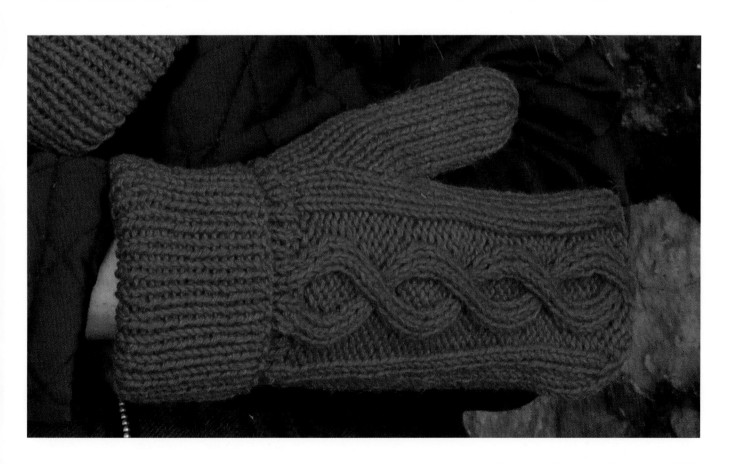

Working on these 17 sts only, work 12 rows even in St st beg with a K row.

Next row: K1, *K2tog, rep from * to end—9 sts. Break off yarn leaving a long end, thread through rem sts, pull up tightly and fasten off. Join thumb seam.

With RS facing, pick up and K2 sts from base of thumb, K3, P2, work Row 7 of chart B over next 12 sts, P2, K3—43 sts.

Next row (WS): P3, K2, work Row 8 of chart B over next 12 sts, K2, P24.

Next row: K24, P2, work Row 9 of chart B over next 12 sts, P2, K3.

Next row: P3, K2, work Row 10 of chart B over next 12 sts, K2, P24.

The last 2 rows set chart B and St st either side.

Working appropriate rows of chart B, work 20 more rows in patt, ending with RS facing for next row.

Shape top

Row 1 [RS]: K1, skpo, K16, K2tog, K1, skpo, P2, work Row 7 of chart B over next 12 sts, P2, K2tog, K1—39 sts.

Row 2: P2, K2, work Row 8 of chart B over next 12 sts, K2, P21.

Row 3: K1, skpo, K14, K2tog, K1, skpo, P1, work Row 9 of chart B over next 12 sts, P1, K2tog, K1—35 sts.

Row 4: P1, P2tog, work Row 10 of chart B over next 12 sts, P2tog tbl, P1, P2 tog, P12, P2tog tbl, P1—31 sts.

Row 5: K1, skpo, K10, K2tog, K1, skpo, P2, C6F, P2, K2tog, K1—27 sts.

Row 6: P1, P2tog, K1, P6, K1, P2tog tbl, K1, P2tog, P8, P2tog tbl, P1—23 sts.

Bind off in patt.

FOR BOTH MITTENS

FINISHING

Join top and side seams, reversing sewing for turnback of cuff.

KEY

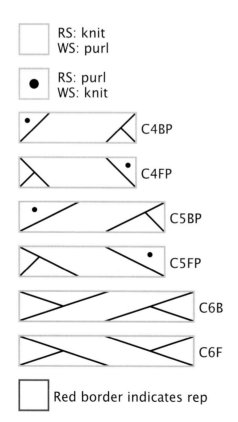

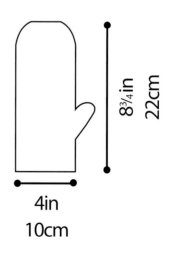

CLASSIC CABLED MITTENS CHART A

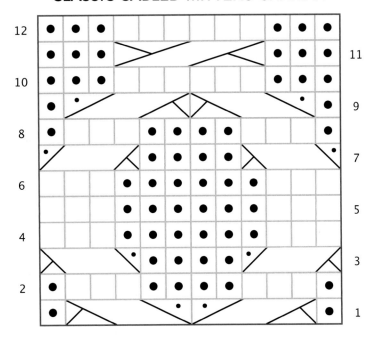

CLASSIC CABLED MITTENS CHART B

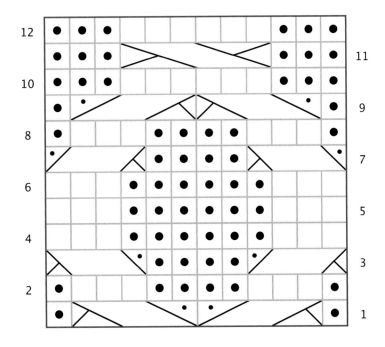

CLASSIC SHRUG

Skill Level ★

MEASUREMENTS AND YARN

Size	32–34 81.5–86.5	36–38 91.5–96.5	40–42 101.5–106.5	in cm
Full Length (approximately)	24 61	25 63.5	26 66	in cm
Width (approximately)	35½ 90	39½ 100.5	43½ 110.5	in cm
Cascade Yarns® (100% Peruvian Highland Wool) Magnum in #9565 Sphere	2	3	3	8$^{4/5}$oz/250g 123yds/112m hanks

OTHER MATERIALS

• 1 pair US 15 (10mm) knitting needles OR SIZE TO OBTAIN GAUGE

• Cable needle

Gauge: 8 sts and 10 rows = 4in/10cm over cable pattern using US 15 (10mm) needles.

TAKE TIME TO CHECK GAUGE.

SPECIAL ABBREVIATIONS

C4B: Slip next 2 sts onto a cable needle and hold at back, K2, then K2 from cable needle.

C4F: Slip next 2 sts onto a cable needle and hold at front, K2, then K2 from cable needle.

C4BP: Slip next 2 sts onto a cable needle and hold at back, K2, then P2 from cable needle.

C4FP: Slip next 2 sts onto a cable needle and hold at front, P2, then K2 from cable needle.

SHRUG

Cast on 34 (36, 38) sts.

Row 1 (RS): K6 (7, 8), P2, *K3, P2, rep from * to last 6 (7, 8) sts, K6 (7, 8).

Row 2: K4 (5, 6), P2, K2, *P3, K2, rep from * to last 6 (7, 8) sts, P2, K4 (5, 6).

The last 2 rows set rib and 4 (5, 6) sts in Gst at each end.

Work even as set for 30 more rows, ending with RS facing for next row.

Inc row: K6 (7, 8), [Pfb] twice, *K1, Kfb, K1, [Pfb] twice, rep from * to last 6 (7, 8) sts, K6 (7, 8)—48 (50, 52) sts.

Row 1 (RS): K4 (5, 6), work Row 1 of chart over next 40 sts, K4 (5, 6).

Row 2: K4 (5, 6), work Row 2 of chart over next 40 sts, K4 (5, 6).

The last 2 rows set chart and Gst at either side.

Work 41 (49, 57) more rows as set, working appropriate rows of chart, ending with Row 3 of chart and WS facing for next row.

Dec row (WS): K6 (7, 8), [P2tog] twice, *K1, K2tog, K1, [P2tog] twice, rep from * to last 6 (7, 8) sts, K6 (7, 8)—34 (36, 38) sts.

Row 1 (RS): K4 (5, 6), P2, K2, *P3, K2, rep from * to last 6 (7, 8) sts, P2, K4 (5, 6).

Row 2: K6 (7, 8), P2, *K3, P2, rep from * to last 6 (7, 8) sts, K6 (7, 8).

The last 2 rows set ribbing and 4 sts in Gst at each end.

Work as set for 30 more rows, ending with RS facing for next row.

Bind off in patt.

FINISHING

Join row end edges of first 32 rows to form sleeve, reversing seam for the first 18 rows for cuff. Join row ends of last 32 rows in the same way to form other sleeve.

KEY

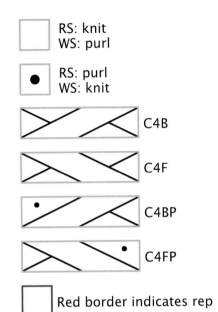

☐ RS: knit
   WS: purl

☒ RS: purl
   WS: knit

C4B

C4F

C4BP

C4FP

☐ Red border indicates rep

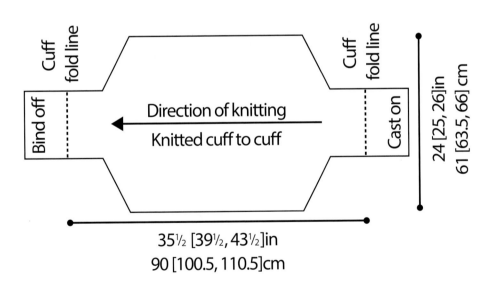

Cuff fold line

Bind off

Cuff fold line

Cast on

Direction of knitting

Knitted cuff to cuff

24 [25, 26]in
61 [63.5, 66] cm

35½ [39½, 43½]in
90 [100.5, 110.5]cm

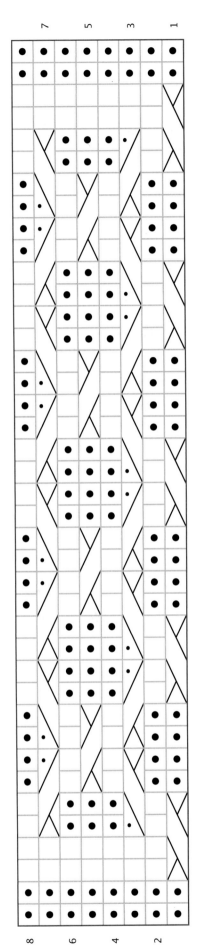

CLASSIC SHRUG CHART

CLASSIC CABLED SCARF

Skill Level ★★

MEASUREMENTS AND YARN

Size	One size only	
Width (approximately)	8 20.5	in cm
Full Length (approximately)	88 223.5	in cm
Debbie Bliss Cashmerino Aran (53% wool, 33% acrylic, 12% cashmere) in #101 Ecru	8	1¾oz/50g 98yds/90m balls

OTHER MATERIALS

• 1 pair US 8 (5mm) knitting needles OR SIZE TO OBTAIN GAUGE

• Cable needle

Gauge: 18 sts and 21 rows = 4in/10cm in St st using US 8 (5mm) needles.

TAKE TIME TO CHECK GAUGE.

SPECIAL ABBREVIATIONS

C4BP: Slip next st onto a cable needle and hold at back, K3, then P1 from cable needle.

C4FP: Slip next 3 sts onto a cable needle and hold at front, P1, then K3 from cable needle.

C6B: Slip next 3 sts onto a cable needle and hold at back, K3, then K3 from cable needle.

C6F: Slip next 3 sts onto a cable needle and hold at front, K3, then K3 from cable needle.

C6BP: Slip next 3 sts onto a cable needle and hold at back, K3, then P3 from cable needle.

C6FP: Slip next 3 sts onto a cable needle and hold at front, P3, then K3 from cable needle.

SCARF

Using US 8 (5mm) needles, cast on 68 sts.

Work from chart until all 16 rows have been repeated a total of 29 times, ending with RS facing for next row.

Bind off.

FINISHING

Weave in all loose ends.

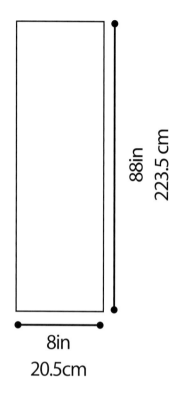

88in
223.5 cm

8in
20.5cm

KEY

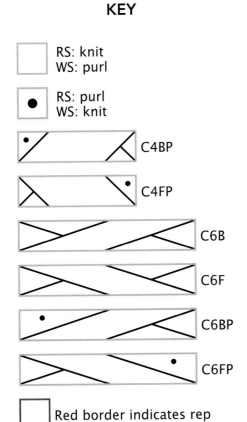

| | RS: knit
WS: purl |
| • | RS: purl
WS: knit |

C4BP

C4FP

C6B

C6F

C6BP

C6FP

Red border indicates rep

CLASSIC CABLED SCARF CHART

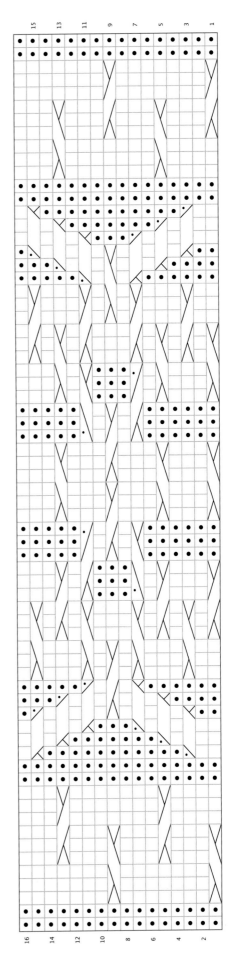

WAISTCOAT

Skill Level ★★

MEASUREMENTS AND YARN

To fit bust	32 81.5	34 86.5	36 91.5	38 96.5	40 101.5	42 106.5	in cm
Actual size	34 86.5	36 91.5	38 96.5	40½ 103	43 109	45 114	in cm
Full Length (approximately)	20½ 52	21¼ 54	21¾ 55	22 56	22¾ 58	23¾ 60.5	in cm
Knoll Yarns© Coast DK (55% lambswool, 45% cotton) in #076 Passion Flower	6	7	7	8	9	9	1¾oz/50g 128yds/117m balls

OTHER MATERIALS

• 1 pair US 3 (3.25mm) knitting needles OR SIZE TO OBTAIN GAUGE

• 1 pair US 6 (4mm) knitting needles OR SIZE TO OBTAIN GAUGE

• 1 US 3 (3.25mm) 32in/81.5cm circular needle OR SIZE TO OBTAIN GAUGE

• Cable needle

• Stitch holders

• Stitch markers

• Shawl pin to fasten

Gauge: 21 sts and 28 rows = 4in/10cm in St st using US 6 (4mm) needles.

TAKE TIME TO CHECK GAUGE.

SPECIAL ABBREVIATIONS

C4B: Slip next 2 sts onto a cable needle and hold at back, K2, then K2 from cable needle.

C4F: Slip next 2 sts onto a cable needle and hold at front, K2, then K2 from cable needle.

C8B: Slip next 4 sts onto a cable needle and hold at back, K4, then K4 from cable needle.

C8F: Slip next 4 sts onto a cable needle and hold at front, K4, then K4 from cable needle.

M1K: Pick up loop between last and next st and knit into the back of this loop to make a st.

M1P: Pick up loop between last and next st and purl into the back of this loop to make a st.

WAISTCOAT

BACK

Using smaller needles cast on 93 (99, 105, 111, 117, 123) sts.

Work 2 rows in Gst.

Change to larger needles.

Beg with a K row, work 86 (88, 88, 88, 90, 94) rows in St st, ending with RS facing for next row.

Place a marker at each end of last row to mark start of armholes.

Work 56 (60, 62, 64, 68, 70) more rows in St st, beg with a K row.

Shape shoulders and back neck

Bind off 10 (11, 12, 13, 14, 15) sts at beg of next 2 rows—73 (77, 81, 85, 89, 93) sts.

Bind off 10 (11, 12, 13, 14, 15) sts at beg of next row, K until there are 14 (15, 16, 16, 17, 18) sts on right hand needle, place rem sts on a holder. Turn.

Work each side of neck separately.

Bind off 3 sts at beg of next row.

Bind off rem 11 (12, 13, 13, 14, 15) sts.

With RS facing, place sts from holder on a needle. Rejoin yarn, bind off center 25 (25, 25, 27, 27, 27) sts, K to end.

Work as for first side, reversing shapings.

LEFT FRONT

Using smaller needles cast on 46 (49, 52, 55, 58, 61) sts.

Work 2 rows in Gst.

Change to larger needles.

Foundation Row 1 (RS): K21 (24, 27, 30, 33, 36), P2, K2, P2, K13, P2, K4.

Foundation Row 2: K2, Pfb twice, K2, Pfb, [P1, Pfb] 6 times, K2, Pfb twice, K2, P21 (24, 27, 30, 33, 36)—57 (60, 63, 66, 69, 72) sts.

NOTE: Work all inc sts in St st.

Row 1 (RS): K21 (24, 27, 30, 33, 36) P2, C4B, P2, K20, P2, C4F, K2.

Row 2: K2, P4, K2, P20, K2, P4, K2, P21 (24, 27, 30, 33, 36).

Row 3: K21 (24, 27, 30, 33, 36), m1K, P2, K4, P2, C8B twice, K4, P2, K6—58 (61, 64, 67, 70, 73) sts.

Row 4: K2, P4, K2, P20, K2, P4, K2, P22 (25, 28, 31, 34, 37).

Row 5: K22 (25, 28, 31, 34, 37), P2, C4B, P2, K20, P2, C4F, K2.

Row 6: K2, P4, K2, P20, K2, P4, K2, m1P, P22 (25, 28, 31, 34, 37)—59 (62, 65, 68, 71, 74) sts.

Row 7: K23 (26, 29, 32, 35, 38), P2, K4, P2, K20, P2, K6.

Row 8: K2, P4, K2, P20, K2, P4, K2, P23 (26, 29, 32, 35, 38).

Row 9: K23 (26, 29, 32, 35, 38), m1K, P2, C4B, P2, K4, C8F twice, P2, C4F, K2—60 (63, 66, 69, 72, 75) sts.

Row 10: K2, P4, K2, P20, K2, P4, K2, P24 (27, 30, 33, 36, 39).

Row 11: K24 (27, 30, 33, 36, 39), P2, K4, P2, K20, P2, K6.

Row 12: K2, P4, K2, P20, K2, P4, K2, m1P, P24 (27, 30, 33, 36, 39)—61 (64, 67, 70, 73, 76) sts.

The last 12 rows set the position of the St st section, the cable panel, and 2 sts in Gst for front edge.

Continuing as set, work 27 (21, 21, 21, 15, 3) rows, inc 1 st as before on every 3rd row, working all inc sts in St st—70 (71, 74, 77, 78, 77) sts.

Work 47 (55, 55, 55, 63, 79) rows, inc 1 st as before on every 4th row, working all inc sts in St st—81 (84, 87, 90, 93, 96) sts.

Place a marker at side edge of last row to mark the start of armhole.

Work 6 rows, inc 1 st as before on next and following 4th row, ending with RS facing for next row, working all inc sts in St st—83 (86, 89, 92, 95, 98) sts.

Shape neck

Next row (RS): K to last 36 sts, slip rem 36 sts to a st holder—47 (50, 53, 56, 59, 62) sts.

Next row: P.

Next row: K to last 4 sts, k2tog, K2—46 (49, 52, 55, 58, 61) sts.

Next row: P.

The last 2 rows set neck decs.

Work 24 (24, 24, 22, 22, 22) rows, dec 1 st at neck edge as before on next, then every other row—34 (37, 40, 44, 47, 50) sts.

Work 17 (21, 21, 27, 29, 33) rows, dec 1 st at neck edge as before on 5th (5th, 5th, 3rd, 5th, next] row, then every 6th (8th, 8th, 6th, 6th, 8th) row. 2 (2, 2, 4, 4, 4) times more—31 (34, 37, 39, 42, 45) sts.

Beg with a P row, work in St st for 5 (5, 7, 5, 7, 5) rows, ending with RS facing for next row.

Shape shoulder

Bind off 10 (11, 12, 13, 14, 15) sts at beg of next row—21 (23, 25, 26, 28, 30) sts.

P 1 row.

Bind off 10 (11, 12, 13, 14, 15) sts at beg of next row—11 (12, 13, 13, 14, 15) sts.

P 1 row.

Bind off rem 11 (12, 13, 13, 14, 15) sts.

RIGHT FRONT

Using smaller needles cast on 46 (49, 52, 55, 58, 61) sts.

Work 2 rows in Gst.

Change to larger needles.

Foundation Row 1 (RS): K4, P2, K13, P2, K2, P2, K21 (24, 27, 30, 33, 36).

Foundation Row 2: P21 (24, 27, 30, 33, 36), K2, Pfb twice, K2, Pfb, [P1, Pfb] 6 times, K2, Pfb twice, K2—57 (60, 63, 66, 69, 72) sts.

NOTE: Work all inc sts in St st.

Row 1 (RS): K2, C4B, P2, K20, P2, C4F, P2, K21 (24, 27, 30, 33, 36).

Row 2: P21 (24, 27, 30, 33, 36), K2, P4, K2, P20, K2, P4, K2.

Row 3: K6, P2, K4, C8F twice, P2, K4, P2, m1K, K21 (24, 27, 30, 33, 36)—58 (61, 64, 67, 70, 73) sts.

Row 4: P22 (25, 28, 31, 34, 37), K2, P4, K2, P20, K2, P4, K2.

Row 5: K2, C4B, P2, K20, P2, C4F, P2, K22 (25, 28, 31, 34, 37).

Row 6: P22 (25, 28, 31, 34, 37), m1P, K2, P4, K2, P20, K2, P4, K2—59 (62, 65, 68, 71, 74) sts.

Row 7: K6, P2, K20, P2, K4, P2, K23 (26, 29, 32, 35, 38).

Row 8: P23 (26, 29, 32, 35, 38), K2, P4, K2, P20, K2, P4, K2.

Row 9: K2, C4B, P2, C8B twice, K4, P2, C4F, P2, m1K, K23 (26, 29, 32, 35, 38)—60 (63, 66, 69, 72, 75) sts.

Row 10: P24 (27, 30, 33, 36, 39), K2, P4, K2, P20, K2, P4, K2.

Row 11: K6, P2, K20, P2, K4, P2, K24 (27, 30, 33, 36, 39).

Row 12: P24 (27, 30, 33, 36, 39), m1P, K2, P4, K2, P20, K2, P4, K2—61 (64, 67, 70, 73, 76) sts.

The last 12 rows set the position of the St st section, the cable panel, and 2 sts in Gst for front edge.

Continuing as set, work 27 (21, 21, 21, 15, 3) rows, inc 1 st as before every 3rd row, working all inc sts in St st—70 (71, 74, 77, 78, 77) sts.

Work 47 (55, 55, 55, 63, 79) rows, inc 1 st as before on every 4th row, working all inc sts in St st—81 (84, 87, 90, 93, 96) sts.

Place a marker at side edge on last row to mark the start of armhole.

Work 6 rows, inc 1 st as before on next and foll 4th row, ending with RS facing for next row, working all inc sts in St st—83 (86, 89, 92, 95, 98) sts.

Shape neck

Next row (RS): Work 36 sts in patt, then slip the sts just worked to a st holder, K to end—47 (50, 53, 56, 59, 62) sts.

Next row: P.

Next row: K2, skpo, K to end—46 (49, 52, 55, 58, 61) sts.

Next row: P.

The last 2 rows set neck decs.

Work 24 (24, 24, 22, 22, 22) rows, dec 1 st at neck edge as before on next and every other row—34 (37, 40, 44, 47, 50) sts.

Work 17 (21, 21, 27, 29, 33) rows, dec 1 st at neck edge as before on 5th (5th, 5th, 3rd, 5th, next] row, then every 6th (8th, 8th, 6th, 6th, 8th) row, 2 (2, 2, 4, 4, 4) times more—31 (34, 37, 39, 42, 45) sts.

Beg with a P row, work 4 (4, 6, 4, 6, 4) rows in St st, ending with WS facing for next row.

Shape shoulder

Bind off 10 (11, 12, 13, 14, 15) sts at beg of next row.

K 1 row.

Bind off 10 (11, 12, 13, 14, 15) sts at beg of next row—11 (12, 13, 13, 14, 15) sts.

K 1 row.

Bind off rem 11 (12, 13, 13, 14, 15) sts.

NECKBAND

Join both shoulder seams.

With RS facing, using circular needle and starting at neck edge of right front pick up and K47 (51, 53, 54, 58, 60) sts evenly along right side of neck, 3 sts down right side of back neck, 26 (26, 26, 28, 28, 28) sts from 25 (25, 25, 27, 27, 27) bound-off sts, 3 sts up left side of back neck, 47 (51, 53, 54, 58, 60) sts evenly along left side of neck and, with RS facing, work in patt across 36 sts left on st holder at left front—162 (170, 174, 178, 186, 190) sts.

Row 1 (WS): Work 36 sts in patt, *P2, K2, rep from * to last 2 sts, P2, and with WS facing, work in patt across 36 sts left on st holder at right front—198 (206, 210, 214, 222, 226) sts.

Row 2: Work 36 sts in patt, K2, *P2, K2, rep from * to last 36 sts, work 36 sts in patt.

Row 3: Work 36 sts in patt, P2, *K2, P2, rep from * to last 36 sts, work 36 sts in patt.

The last 2 rows form rib and cable placement.

Work even as set for a further 6 rows, ending with RS facing for next row.

Next row: K2, K2tog twice, P2, [K2tog, K1] 6 times, K2tog, P2, K2tog twice, *P2, K2, rep from * to last 36 sts, P2, K2tog twice, P2, [K2tog, K1] 6 times, K2tog, P2, K2tog twice, K2—176 (184, 188, 192, 200, 204) sts.

Next row: K25, P2, *K2, P2, rep from * to last 25 sts, K25.

Next row: K27, P2, *K2, P2, rep from * to last 27 sts, K27.

Bind off in patt.

ARMHOLE BORDERS

With RS facing, using smaller needles pick up and K76 (82, 86, 88, 94, 98] sts evenly between markers.

Work 2 rows in Gst, ending with WS facing for next row.

Bind off on WS as if to knit.

FINISHING

Join side and armhole border seams.

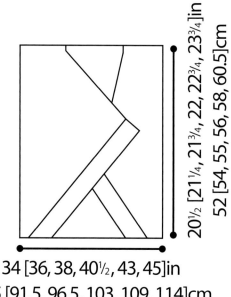

20½ [21¼, 21¾, 22, 22¾, 23¾]in
52 [54, 55, 56, 58, 60.5]cm

34 [36, 38, 40½, 43, 45]in
86.5 [91.5, 96.5, 103, 109, 114]cm

ABBREVIATIONS

beg	begin/beginning
cm	centimeter(s)
cont	continue/continued
dec	decrease/decreased/decreases/decreasing
dpn	double-pointed needle(s)
foll	follow/follows/following
g	gram
Gst	garter stitch
in	inch(es)
inc	increase/increased/increases/increasing
K	knit
K2tog	knit 2 sts tog
Kfb	knit into front and back of next stitch
mm	millimeters
m	marker
m	meters (in materials list only)
m1	make one: increase by picking up horizontal loop lying before next st and working into the back of it
oz	ounce
P	purl
P2tog	purl 2 sts tog
patt	pattern
patt2tog	working in pattern, work 2 sts together
Pfb	purl into front and back of next stitch
pm	place marker
psso	pass slipped stitch over
rem	remain/remaining
rep	repeat(s), repeating
Rev St st	reverse stockinette stitch
rib	work in ribbing
rib2tog	work 2 sts together in ribbing
RS	right side of work
skpo	slip 1, K1, pass slip st over
sl	slip
sl st	slip stitch(es)
sm	stitch marker
st(s)	stitch(es)
St st	stockinette st
tbl	through back of loop(s)
tog	together
WS	wrong side of work
yds	yards
yo	yarn over

NEEDLE CONVERSION

US	UK
US–UK CONVERSION	
0	2.00
1	2.25
–	2.50
2	2.75
2	3.00
3	3.25
4	3.50
5	3.75
6	4.00
7	4.50
8	5.00
9	5.50
10	6.00
10.5	6.50
–	7.00
–	7.50
11	8.00
13	9.00
15	10.00

ABOUT THE AUTHOR

Jody Long was born in Portsmouth, in the United Kingdom, in 1984. He grew up in Waterlooville, Hampshire, and moved to Malaga, Spain, in 2014. For over twelve years he designed for all of the major UK and US knitting magazines, then moved on to design for knitting mills around the globe. Jody has also designed for celebrity clients. Jody has his own yarn called "Easy Care."